The Joy *of* Planning

Designing Minilesson Cycles in Grades 3–6

Franki Sibberson

CHOICELITERACY

Choice Literacy, P.O. Box 790, Holden, Maine 04429
www.choiceliteracy.com

Copyright © 2012 by Franki Sibberson

Library of Congress Cataloging in Publication Data Pending

ISBN 978-1-60155-037-8

Cover and interior design by Martha Drury
Manufactured in the United States of America

16 15 14 13 12   10 9 8 7 6 5 4 3 2 1

CONTENTS

Video and Print Bonuses
To view free video and print supplements for this
book, visit www.choiceliteracy.com and click on the
"Books and DVDs" link on the homepage.

The Joy *of* Planning

Planning: The Heart of Teaching

My mother and I are both planners. We overthink every detail. Whether we are planning a small family brunch or a large wedding, we pay close attention to every aspect of the preparation.

In 1988 I married my husband, Scott. Although he is not Italian, we had a big Italian wedding complete with the traditional Italian cookie table. I loved my wedding, but I enjoyed the planning almost as much. One of my most vivid memories of planning was the cake selection. Several months before the wedding, we were celebrating a family birthday. My mother decided that the birthday provided the perfect opportunity to try out some of the bakeries she had visited for the wedding cake. So, on this birthday, my mother showed up with SIX birthday cakes—each from different local (and not-so-local) bakeries. Our job at the birthday party was to try each cake and decide which tasted better. She had already determined that each of the bakeries met the expectations she had for what the cake would *look* like, but she wanted to make sure we had a wedding cake that not only looked good, but tasted good as well, and of course, was a cake that I liked. After all,

I was the bride—the reason for the planning—so my input was key. Needless to say, all of the wedding cakes were delicious and we ended up with a good one.

I admit that the cake selection process was a little extreme, but to me, this was a clear picture of how the details of the wedding had to be just right in order to match the vision we had for the event. We had to have a vision for the wedding, but the planning and the little decisions made the whole event come to life. I put the time into the planning and loved every minute of it, because I was preparing for a joyful event.

In some ways, planning cycles of minilessons takes me back to the care and energy I put into my wedding planning. It takes time, but it is worth every minute. There is little that brings me more joy than thinking through students, books, and what might be learned in my classroom. But if I am perfectly honest, I have to admit it wasn't always this way.

Falling Back in Love with Lesson Planning

For a while, minilessons didn't seem to fit into my bigger goals of the reading workshop. I realized a few years ago that I was often going through the motions of minilesson work—using the time at the beginning of reading workshop to "share" content with students. I was spending more time thinking about what I would "do" in the minilesson work than worrying about the thinking and learning the students would do. I realized I had never really stepped back to think about what it was I believed about the minilesson part of the workshop and whether my beliefs were matching my practice.

I had to sit back and reflect on my beliefs. I had to force myself to really stop and think about what it was I wanted from my minilessons. What were my big goals for the minilesson portion of the reading workshop? Did I merely want to give myself a pat on the back for "covering" curriculum? Did I spend more time thinking about the chart we would create than the ways kids might use what I was teaching in their own reading? Most important, who owned the minilesson work, the students or me?

Although I had spent years thinking hard about the whole of reading workshop, I had never really thought hard about these things as they related specifically to my work with minilessons. I knew what the minilesson portion of the workshop would look like to a teacher visiting my classroom, but I began to think about them from the students' perspective. What messages do minilessons give to students in the classroom? Do these messages match my bigger goals for reading workshop?

Much of the professional literature is focused on what teachers "do" during minilessons rather than the role we play. The emphasis is on management, time limits, and content. The things that are most important to me about minilesson work are not so much what I do or the content that I give to students, but the patterns of thinking that I help my students develop independently.

Taking time to identify my beliefs has helped me stay grounded when I am in the planning process. Minilessons are powerful routines that build student independence. Although this understanding makes the planning process much more challenging, being clear about my beliefs helps me stay true to my larger mission of developing independent readers. Here is what I believe about minilessons:

1. Minilessons should be designed with a vision of helping students gain the necessary skills, strategies, and behaviors to become independent readers.

As a high school English student, I listened to lectures, took good notes in class, and passed the tests on every book. My English teacher taught about themes in books, the ways in which characters changed, and symbolism. It never once occurred to me that there were strategies I could learn that would help me read for these things on my own. I did not know that I could interact with the text and make meaning. I just assumed that the teacher's understanding was the only possible meaning. I had no idea that I could make meaning on my own.

I believe that minilessons should empower students and help them develop strong identities as readers. As Peter Johnston reminds us in *Choice Words*, "Building an identity means coming to see in ourselves the characteristics of particular categories (and roles) of people and developing a sense of what it feels like to be that sort of person and belong in certain social spaces" (2004, 23). Each minilesson or minilesson cycle should open up possibilities for ways in which students can make meaning.

2. Minilessons should be scaffolded across time to deepen and enrich understanding of concepts. They are not activities delivered in isolation.

Minilessons should build on where kids are, not where they aren't. The testing environment has trained teachers to look at the things a student cannot do. Although that is important for some student needs, I find that for daily planning purposes, I can teach for deeper understanding if I build from what the students do know and what they can do.

Minilesson work should also be scaffolded across a cycle. Designing cycles so that the concepts are most accessible to students is key. Then we move slowly and explicitly beyond that beginning point to help children understand at deeper levels. Planning high-quality minilessons involves not only thinking about the lessons themselves, but ordering the lessons in ways that make the most sense to students.

Finally, I believe that we must scaffold lessons across grade levels. Because readers deal with the same concepts, strategies, and behaviors across their lives as readers, we need to help them add depth to their reading year by year. We don't want an inferring study to look exactly the same in second grade as it does in fifth grade. Scaffolding across content is not only about providing harder and more complex texts, but also about helping readers think more deeply with these skills. The Common Core Standards help—they give a framework in which to think about how understanding builds from year to year.

3. Minilessons should be part of larger conversations that we as a community have about our reading lives and that these conversations build over time.

Max Brand, author of *Word Savvy*, helped me see the work of minilessons as an ongoing conversation within a community of readers. This conversation begins on the first day of school and continues through the year. We never *finish* a topic. For instance, if we end a lesson cycle on inferring, that doesn't mean that we are finished talking about inferences. What we understand about inferring becomes part of all future learning. Each minilesson adds to the ways our classroom community can think and talk about books.

4. Minilessons should be interactive. Students should be the ones doing the thinking, not the teacher.

A while ago, I realized that I had been taking too much control of minilesson work—I was the only one talking and thinking. It was the only chance I had to pull the whole group together and *teach* something, and was the part of workshop that felt traditional. Then I realized that not only was I the only one talking, but I was also the only one interacting with the text. I was talking *at* my children. I knew that if I wanted students to control their reading lives, I needed to let go of the notion that I was imparting knowledge. I realized that minilessons need to be interactive in nature, and that it was the students who needed to be the ones doing the thinking and interacting.

Even though the minilesson work is often thought of as the "explicit teaching time" in the reader's workshop, the ways in which we run these lessons give our students messages about what is valued in the classroom and what it means to be a reader. If the minilesson is a time when I as the teacher do all of the talking and thinking, I am giving my students the message that I am in charge of reading in this classroom. Instead, I want them to own their reading lives and to come to know the power they have as readers. Katie Ray reminds us, "Expert teaching invites students to act with initiative and intention in shaping what happens to them throughout the day" (2006, 60). I want my minilessons to give students this message every day.

5. Minilessons should be planned with the needs of current students in mind. They can't be canned, scripted, or duplicated year after year.

I gave up keeping a filing cabinet years ago. Early in my teaching career, I discovered that repeating the same lessons year after year did not yield the same results with different groups of students. I quickly learned that different groups of children bring different things to each lesson, and I needed to be responsive in my teaching.

Even though the curriculum is similar year after year, the way in which I teach has to vary. I cannot rely on a set of canned, prewritten lessons (whether written by some publisher, by local colleagues, or by me) for my minilessons. Instead I have to take into account what the curriculum tells me about what needs to be taught and connect that to the information I learn from my students about their needs. Of course,

I have resources I refer to, and every so often a "canned" lesson is a perfect fit, but overall, I have to rethink and recreate cycles based on the current students I am teaching.

6. Minilessons should be the right length to match your teaching point. There is no magic number of minutes for an effective minilesson.

Minilessons can be effective only when embedded in an authentic reading workshop, with an emphasis on independent, choice reading. Because independent reading is the key, minilessons can be only a very small part of the reading workshop. Usually this means the minilesson is only 5–10 minutes out of a 45–60-minute block. The lessons work only if students have time to practice what they are learning in texts of their choosing. During reading workshop, the majority of a student's time is spent reading books of his or her choice independently, and the minilesson shouldn't cut into that precious time.

Ideally, I love when my minilessons are seven to ten minutes long, but there are some great minilessons that have happened in two minutes, and others that took much longer than ten minutes. Every so often, we need to have whole-class learning in a larger chunk of time. For me, it is about the patterns of my minilessons. If most of my minilessons are twenty minutes long, I need to rethink the time I am taking away from student independence. I want my students to know that the thing we value most is independent reading time, and that can't happen if too much of our time is spent in minilesson work.

7. Minilessons should be organized in a way that makes the most sense to the teacher, school, or district. There is no one right way to organize lessons.

The minilesson portion of our work is critical, because in a workshop setting, this is the time when the whole group is involved in one conversation. But I don't believe there is one right way to organize teaching. There are many options about which cycles to focus on. Some districts or teachers focus on strategy cycles, whereas others teach through genre. One of the biggest decisions we make as teachers is which long-term lesson cycles to teach. I have found that these lesson cycles are really only the anchors for our planning. Teachers who teach strategy cycles are still talking about literary elements and genre.

Teachers who organize their planning through genre study embed strategy work. The cycle becomes both the umbrella for planning and the vehicle to connect the content.

8. Minilessons should be based on what we know about teaching and learning. Regardless of the mandates and pressures of state testing, there is no reason to compromise best teaching practice. The testing environment has made teaching a bit more challenging as schools move toward pacing guides, mandates, and required lessons. But this is not an excuse to give up what we know about good teaching.

We know what makes a high-quality lesson, and we know when students truly understand a concept. It is important in minilesson planning that we hold on to those things that we know about good teaching. It is tempting to spend an entire year giving students work that "looks like" the mandated test, and to make every assessment one that mimics the state test. It is tempting to teach only the way a concept is tested. But testing and test practice are not teaching.

9. Minilessons should be designed to teach the reader, not the book.
The key to planning, no matter what your limits or mandates, is to work within them to teach the *reader* and not the *book*. Lucy Calkins discusses this in her landmark book *The Art of Teaching Writing*. She writes, "[We] are teaching the writer and not the writing. Our decisions must be guided by 'what might help this writer' rather than 'what might help this writing'" (1994, 228). I believe the exact same thing about readers. I believe that if we remember to keep our focus on readers, and not the book, we can work within any mandates that are given to us.

So often, we want our students to understand a book in the ways we understand it. Often we bring years of experience to books we share with our students. We have read the book as an adult and may have read it with several groups of students. We know the book well, and may force the deep understanding we have of the book (because we have read it so many times) onto our students. This does not allow students to do their own thinking, practice strategies they've learned, and build understanding as they go into a book. I am most concerned that my students be able to use the skills and strategies developed with one text in the future with other texts. I am less worried about whether they know the "correct" theme in Jerry Spinelli's *Wringer* than I am about giving them time to practice ways to find themes so that they can use these skills in all future reading.

10. Minilessons should be designed by the teachers who are doing the teaching, not corporations.
Planning and teaching are complex. Each lesson builds on what a student or group of students brings to it. The teacher is the person who spends time with the students in her care, and is the one best suited to create lessons that will meet her students where they are. Because lessons are designed to help build understanding, it is important that teachers develop the lessons they teach so that they can revise and replan as needed, based on student response.

When we plan, we think about all that we know about our students— their strengths and challenges. We bring in our knowledge of the content as well as our knowledge of child development and learning. The planning process allows us to synthesize for ourselves where to go next.

Identifying my beliefs about minilessons has been an important step for me in learning to plan effectively. Ultimately, I want my students to change and grow as readers, and I have limited time for the minilesson work that will invite this growth. As Michael Fullan says in *Motion Leadership*, it is all about "finding the smallest number of high-leverage, easy to understand actions that unleash stunningly powerful consequences" (2009, 16).

Reclaiming the Joy of Lesson Planning

It is hard these days to remember that teachers are the people who know our students best and that we are the ones who are well equipped to plan lessons that will help them move forward in their learning. We are being made to believe that our students are not doing well, and that we need outsiders (who do not know our students) to come in and help us be successful. The work of planning is being taken away from teachers. Districts are being encouraged to buy programs that are "teacher-proof." Teachers are being asked to stay on the same page or lesson as the teacher next door, regardless of the level of under-standing each teacher's students have.

Many of us are drowning in data. Don't get me wrong . . . I *love* to analyze my students' work and thinking to determine where to go next with their learning. I have spent many Friday nights throughout my career with student work spread across my kitchen table, looking at work samples with an eye toward instruction. Yet we are now some-times forced to spend so much time looking at and analyzing isolated test data that we have no energy left for using the data to plan instruc-tion. The flip side is that when we look to isolated data, we tend to teach isolated skills. I think it is time we put the same amount of time and energy into planning for instruction as we do into analyzing data.

Kelly Gallagher writes in his book *Readacide*, "Standards are critical in helping teachers plan and align their instruction. If the powers-that-be took away every mandated test tomorrow, I would still want to know the state's definition of good teaching. I would continue to read the standards carefully, with an eye for preparing meaningful lessons for my students. Standards are necessary, and having them has made me a better teacher" (2009, 9). I agree with Kelly. When we know where we need to focus our teaching and what our students need, then the hard work of planning and the important work of teaching can happen.

Lesson plan books have not changed much since I began teaching. I imagine they haven't changed much since the beginning of time. For years, we have been asked to think in terms of individual days and les-sons—to fit our lessons into small boxes. Although we plan with a vision in mind, the daily lesson planning sometimes goes against big-picture planning. The problem with daily lesson planning is that the process invites planning without the guide of a vision. Lessons can easily turn into unconnected "activities" instead of interconnected building blocks that lead to something bigger.

In contrast to the concept of isolated daily lesson plans there was a time in the 1980s when we learned big-picture planning through what we called "integrated units." These thematic units had a good premise. Learning had to be connected for students. If it wasn't, it didn't make sense to them. I learned a lot by thinking about how to connect skills and content in a lesson cycle. The missing ingredient in this type of planning for me was that the connecting topic was also one that was randomly selected. Common themes in the 1980s were teddy bears, ladybugs, or pumpkins. We connected everything we knew about the topic to the unit, without focusing on a few key concepts or skills we wanted students to come away with.

If we can combine all that we know about thematic units of study with the understanding we have of standards-based teaching, we can create powerful learning experiences for our students. The key is to use standards to rebuild focused, integrated cycles and to think about the ways these cycles build on one another and are revisited throughout the school year. The cycle is the vehicle through which to deliver the standards and curriculum. Thoughtful planning is the day-to-day thinking that needs to go into the implementation.

I plan best when I think about planning as a bridge between standards, curriculum, and student learning. And I have come to see how I need both a big-picture vision and daily lesson plans that look at smaller chunks of time.

Regardless of the mandates, we can change our stance so that we look beyond daily plans and instead are intentional about how individual lessons build to something bigger. As Debbie Miller reminds us, "Intentional teachers are thoughtful, reflective people who are conscious of the decisions they make and the actions they take; they live and teach by the principles and practices they value and believe in" (2008, 4).

Lesson planning is truly one of the most important and joyful things we do as teachers.

What to Expect from the Rest of the Book

The remainder of this book is an attempt to make my minilesson planning visible. I certainly don't have all the answers, but I do love planning and seeing the learning that happens when planning is thoughtful and designed with specific students and learning goals in mind.

Each chapter looks at one particular focus through a cycle of lessons. These cycles are not intended to be stand-alone units that you can use tomorrow with any class. Instead, let them serve as a starting point for your own planning.

I hope that by making the thinking behind my planning more visible, I can help teachers regain confidence in their planning skills while continuing to meet the mandates that are placed before us.

CHAPTER 1

Planning *the* First Minilesson Cycles *of the* Year

Learning is not about one great lesson or one great activity teachers design for students to do. It is about the little things teachers ask students to do every day like read, write, and talk, that add up to the big things like making meaning from text and adding meaning and purpose to life.

—Samantha Bennett, *That Workshop Book*

I was lucky enough to visit the Manhattan New School in New York City when Shelley Harwayne was principal. It was there that I saw Sharon Taberski, Joanne Hindley, and Judy Davis in action. I have also benefited from watching videos of amazing teachers such as Debbie Miller, Stephanie Harvey, Cris Tovani, and Aimee Buckner as they taught minilessons to their students.

Every time I watched these teachers in action through video, I was inspired by what I saw. Students were reading independently. They could talk to each other about books with depth. They had favorite authors and genres. The students seemed to value their reading lives, and it was this ownership that allowed them to access the curriculum successfully. Watching master teachers work alongside students has provided some of my most powerful learning. These teachers helped me create a vision for my teaching.

What I discovered was that good teaching is rarely about one lesson or series of lessons. I recently revisited one of the best classroom videos I know, with Debbie Miller teaching from *The Royal Bee* by Frances and Ginger Park. I remember watching this video for the first time and wanting so badly for that lesson to happen in my classroom. I did everything just like Debbie in that lesson with my students. I created the same charts and used some of Debbie's brilliant language. I did this frequently when I saw videos of lessons that inspired me. But the thing is, the lessons never played out in the same way for my students as they did in the videos. My students often looked at me with blank stares, or jumped in with connections and questions that didn't help us go deeper into the text.

I now realize that Debbie Miller wasn't just teaching a single lesson using *The Royal Bee*. Instead, she knew her students so well that she could guide and scaffold their learning perfectly. Debbie understood what the students would bring to the lesson from previous lessons and from conferring with them individually. She planned this lesson knowing what her students *could* do and built on that. When I watch the video now, it is obvious to me that her students could

- record their thinking,
- support their thinking with evidence,
- understand the concept of theme by listing possibilities of theme,
- build on each other's thinking, and
- make strong connections between books and past learning.

Looking at this list, I am struck by the fact that only one of these skills is directly connected to literary themes—the topic of the lesson. The other strategies and behaviors were linked to the intellectual community that Debbie had built. This type of talk and thinking didn't just happen—she taught these skills, and gave students plenty of time to practice them.

When I jumped in and taught the lesson, using the same book and language that Debbie used, my lesson flopped because my students did not come with the same set of skills, strategies, and behaviors in place. I could not just grab any lesson and teach it successfully.

I have shown videos like this one to teachers in workshop settings, and I find that many of them have had a similar experience. They are inspired, yet frustrated. Their response? "My kids can't do that." At first I worried that teachers did not have high expectations of their students, but I know that isn't the case. Teachers watching experts like Debbie Miller know that their students don't have the skills in place for that level of thinking and talk *right now*. The question then becomes, "What would my students need to be able to do that?" Minilesson planning really begins with knowing where your students are, and moving from there.

More Than Standards

There is a reason why many teachers disagree with the idea of scripted lesson plans and a mandated curriculum. Following a scripted plan that is guaranteed to meet every student's needs sounds easy enough. But with the different needs and strengths that each child brings to the classroom, we know that good teaching cannot happen by following scripted programs and standardizing instruction. To teach the curriculum, we need to know each child well. Good teaching comes from planning with specific students in mind. It is about knowing both our curriculum and our students well. It is also about understanding readers and knowing the things that good readers do. Weaving all of this knowledge together is the only way we can build an intellectual community in the classroom.

The Common Core, or any standards for that matter, give us a goal—what we want our students to be able to do at a certain point in time. What they do not give us are the ways to help our students meet those goals.

Reading strategies and behaviors are the tools that give readers the ability to think deeply about a text. Often we worry about spending valuable class time teaching things that aren't "in the curriculum." But as I think about the power of minilesson work, it is these strategies and behaviors that scaffold all learning for our students. These are the strategies and behaviors that will help students read deeply no matter which genre or topic they are reading, and they work across all standards.

Cycle Planning: Putting the Pieces Together

Sometimes we get to choose the cycles we teach, and other times our district or school dictates what we teach and when we teach it. But the planning process always involves combining what we know about the curriculum with what we know about students. No matter how I decide on a cycle topic, I tend to go through the same thinking process to plan an effective cycle.

I have to make sure that each lesson and cycle helps readers grow from where they are. I have to know books well, and which mentor texts will naturally invite certain types of conversations and learning. I need to have a vision of what I want to happen by the end of the cycle.

Figure 1 **Planning Minilesson Cycles**

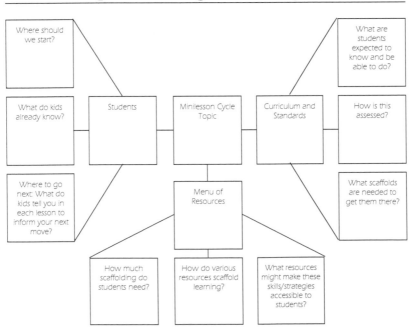

This weaving together is what creates an effective cycle. As Terry Thompson reminds us in his article "Are You Scaffolding or Rescuing?," "True scaffolding takes an in-depth knowledge of readers as well as the instructional practices that will most benefit them, and it involves a seamless, almost art-like dance to the beats of varying levels of support. A dance that is different for each student, and one where the steps can change based on the needs of the reader and the focus of the instruction."

I plan in a way that allows me to back up or move ahead based on what each student brings to the lessons. As Michael J. Fox reminds us in his book *A Funny Thing Happened on the Way to the Future*, "In my experience, a mentor doesn't necessarily tell you what to do, but more importantly, tells you what *they* did or might do, then trusts you to draw your own conclusions and act accordingly. If you succeed they'll take one step back, and if you screw up, they'll take one step closer" (2010, 78).

The First Steps of Cycle Planning

The first step in planning a cycle for me is always to determine the umbrella or topic. In some districts, these topics are already determined for teachers. Teachers are required to teach units or cycles on literary elements or strategies, and there is little choice about the topic of each unit. In other districts, teachers have ownership over how the curriculum is taught, and they can determine the ways in which to organize their units for student learning. I have flexibility in my planning, so my cycle design begins with determining a topic or umbrella for the cycle of study. Across the year, I try to teach using a variety of categories. My cycles of study are balanced between content such as a literary element, behaviors such as book choice, and strategies such as inferring. I want content, behaviors, and strategies to be in the forefront of my students' minds as readers, so I try to balance across the year.

To determine each cycle's umbrella, I look at the curriculum and think about what my students need most at this particular point in time. I try to find one thing that is in my curriculum that students are ready for, and one that will move them forward as readers quickly. Once I determine the cycle umbrella, I have to ask myself these questions and then determine how to best break down the ideas for my students:

How does this cycle fit into the bigger picture of reading?

What are the big goals I have for this study?

What specific curriculum standards will I weave into this cycle of study?

Which books might I use and why?

How will I provide for students to enter at their own level?

What will I be assessing? Does the assessment match the big-picture goal?

In Figure 2, you can see the specific process I go through when designing a cycle of study. I consider three categories: students, curriculum/standards, and resources. I first want to think about students and to synthesize all that they bring to this particular study. Then I want to dig into the curriculum documents to understand exactly what is expected of students at this age. I determine the level of understanding needed and the concepts to be mastered. I think about how best to assess the learning for this particular unit. Finally, I analyze the ways that the available resources will support student learning. I have to think not only about the resources I will use, but about the order in which I'll use them as I think about how they might scaffold learning. I might need some extra resources for students who need more practice.

Let me show you how this cycle works very early in the fall, when I have the handicap of not knowing my students well.

A First Lesson Cycle: Recording Thinking and Responding to Texts

I have the same experience every fall. I listen to student responses to texts, and I worry that they lack some essential skills for comprehending what they are reading. But after so many years of teaching, I understand that this is the work of teaching—figuring out where kids are, and then figuring out how to move them forward. Instead of worrying, I have learned to watch and listen with curiosity to those first conversations I have with students about books. I am listening for patterns in the ways they talk about books. I know that I want students to have the following behaviors, so I listen in to figure out which are in place and which need some time and teaching. These are

Figure 2 **Minilesson Cycles Planning**

Cycle Topic

Thinking While You Read

In order for students to be confident thinking deeply about text, I want them to have experience using tools for talking and recording thinking. These skills will help them with all that we do with comprehension throughout the year.

What are the big goals I have for this study?

student comfort in talking about text
student value listening to and building on others' thinking
recording thinking in a variety of ways
supporting thinking with evidence
noticing confusions while reading
noting changes in thinking while reading

Which books might I use? Why? What types of things am I looking for in books for this cycle?

Variety of books and texts
Nonfiction picture books
Online articles
Essential 55 by Ron Clark (opinions)

How will I provide for students to enter at their own level?

I will share most texts as read alouds first
Talk and written thinking will be equally important

What will I be assessing? Does the assessment match the big picture goals?

I want to assess the growth in the comfort level of recording thinking, sharing thinking, and valuing others' thinking with sticky notes, texts, and conversations.

the behaviors that I know are important for deep understanding of text in grades 3–6:

- Talking to others about text
- Building on someone else's thinking
- Changing your thinking as you read
- Recording thinking as you read
- Stopping to think
- Understanding that reading is thinking
- Supporting thinking with evidence in the text
- Noticing confusion
- Using a variety of tools for annotating text
- Choosing books

I use quick lesson cycles during the first months of school to begin building these essential reading behaviors. I know I must plant the seeds early by showing kids ways to think and talk about texts. I use minilesson time for two to four days to introduce various ideas and behaviors that will be important all year long. Then these strategies and behaviors become embedded in all future minilessons. Figure 2 shows my thinking at the beginning stages of one of these first lesson cycles.

Many of these lesson cycles serve several purposes at the beginning of the school year. Not only can I help students become comfortable with some of the behaviors as readers, but I can also get some informal assessment data from conversations and quick writing responses that help me know where to go next.

The key for me is to teach these skills early in the year without worrying about the content of the piece. Instead, I want to focus on reading behaviors. Later in the year, I may integrate content-related pieces, but early in the year, I can't use a piece that I really want kids to master if my goal is teaching them behaviors and strategies.

For example, when teaching kids to learn to talk about texts, I tend to begin with fun pieces about topics students are interested in, like school uniforms or healthful school lunches. We may go back to these topics later in a social studies unit, but if my goal is strategy or behavior work, I need to stick to that. Of course we talk about the uniforms and our opinions, but I try to focus our talk on the behaviors of readers, giving them time to understand the power of these behaviors.

LESSON **Readers Think in a Variety of Ways When They Read**

I want students to understand that reading is about thinking and that readers think in a variety of ways while they are reading. Sometimes, stopping to think while reading will help them understand the text more clearly. My goal in this cycle is for students to become comfortable noticing and recording their thinking while they read. This first lesson helps me see what they do naturally without much direction.

Possible Anchor Text

I use any short piece of text students will most likely have an opinion about. I often use a chapter from Ron Clark's *Essential 55*, in which Clark speaks of the rules he uses in his classrooms. When we read one of these pieces, students usually have strong feelings one way or another about his rules. I keep my eye out for short articles in the local newspaper or on the Internet that may be of interest to students—articles about school lunches, recess times, or a longer school year. For this text, I am looking for any piece that will spark discussion and that has no right answer. I want students to disagree, discuss, and see that thinking while reading isn't about finding one right answer.

How I Teach It

I hand students each a copy of the piece we'll be sharing. I read the piece aloud, and students have the option of following along. I don't want them to focus on reading the text, so I level the field for readers, regardless of their ability, by reading aloud. Then I give them pencils and ask them to reread the text, marking any of their thinking as they read. I let them know that sometimes readers think before they start to read, sometimes they think as they are reading, and sometimes they think after they finish. Then I send students off for 10 to 12 minutes to record their thinking. After that time, we return to the whole group to share what we noticed.

Questions I Might Ask to Start the Conversation

What did you notice about the kinds of thinking you were doing as you read?

Was it hard or easy to pay attention to your thinking as you read today?

What types of things did you write?

Follow-Up

This lesson informs my teaching immensely as I walk around and see students writing. Because I want to value all and any thinking that students do, I take notes on the types of things I may want to address at a later date. I will follow this lesson up with more opportunities for practice. Using sticky notes, reading notebooks, notebook paper, and other tools, students will gain practice with this strategy across texts.

LESSON **There Are Many Ways to Record Thinking While You Read**

I want readers to understand that the thinking strategies they learn can be transferred to many types of texts and formats.

Possible Anchor Text

A great site for short nonfiction pieces is Wonderopolis (http://wonderopolis.org). This site is filled with interesting things children may wonder about, followed by a detailed answer. Many of the entries also include a video, but I stick to the text for this lesson. I try to find two related pieces—one that I can use to model and one that I can give to kids for practice. My two favorites for this lesson are Wonder #315, "Why Doesn't Glue Stick to the Inside of the Bottle?," and Wonder #309, "How Does an Eraser Work?" Since these are similar topics, they pair well for this lesson.

How I Teach It

I teach this lesson on a screen or interactive whiteboard. I post the article and read it aloud as I note my own thinking. I am intentional about modeling many different types of thinking, focusing on the types that students may not have shared the previous day. I circle unknown words, draw lines to connected ideas, write questions in the margins, and underline places where I am confused. My goal is to model as many types of thinking and recording as possible. When I am finished, I ask students what they noticed about my thinking and what types of things they might try next time they read. I then pass out the second article and invite them to try some new ways to record their thinking.

Questions I Might Ask to Start the Conversation

What kinds of thinking did you notice me doing that you hadn't thought of?

What did you see me do that you might try?

Was today's recording easier or harder than yesterday's? Why?

How did this recording help you as a reader?

Follow-Up

If necessary, we organize the categories of thinking. For example, we could chart the variety of ways we think and/or record our thinking, and then use the chart to post some of our thinking as examples. A chart like this can often serve as an anchor, inviting students to try something new.

LESSON **Using Thinking Tools to Support Understanding**

The purpose of this lesson is twofold. Up until this lesson, students have been recording their thinking by writing directly on a copy of the text. This works early in the cycle, but is not always possible in reading workshop. I want students to see how easy it is to use these same skills with tools such as sticky notes.

Different tools also invite different ways of thinking. We all love new tools, and if I can give students tools they love using, they will find creative ways to meet the goals of the lesson.

This lesson opens up new possibilities for students.

Possible Anchor Text

Any short article will do for this lesson. I tend to find an article with both text and visuals, because we have focused solely on text until this time. Some great sources for short nonfiction text for this lesson are *National Geographic for Kids* and *Sports Illustrated for Kids*. Both of these children's magazines do an incredible job of combining text and visuals in their articles.

How I Teach It

I introduce a basket of tools to students, including highlighters, colored pencils, large sticky notes, arrow-shaped sticky notes, small sticky notes, and highlighter tape. I quickly share how each tool works, and talk about how they could be used to record thinking. As I hold each one up and demonstrate how it works, I ask for ideas from the class on what kind of thinking they might record with a tool like this. Then they get to work, using the tools to record thinking. We gather together to talk about the tools after about ten minutes of independent reading and recording time.

Questions I Might Ask to Start the Conversation

Did the tools help you understand the text? How?

What did these tools allow you to do that you hadn't been able to do before when recording your thinking?

Did you notice that some tools worked better for different things?

What are some new things you noticed about your thinking today?

Follow-Up

I introduce other new tools one at a time after this lesson so that students become comfortable recording thinking in a variety of ways.

LESSON Transferring Recording Skills to Personal Reading

I want students to know that thinking occurs no matter when or where you are reading. Recording thinking will help them understand any text they are reading more deeply.

Possible Anchor Text

There is no anchor text for this lesson. Instead, I have students use the book they are currently reading independently during reading workshop time. I want to give students time to monitor and record their thinking in the book they are currently reading.

How I Teach It

I begin this lesson by asking students to bring the book they are currently reading to the meeting area. I give them each a pack of sticky notes and a pencil and remind them of all the thinking we've done over the last few days. I then ask them to go off and record some of their thinking as they read. I let them know that sometimes it is harder in longer fiction books to notice thinking, and that we'll give it a try today. We then go off on our own for 10 to 12 minutes and come back as a whole group to discuss the kinds of thinking we recorded.

Questions I Might Ask to Start the Conversation

How was this type of thinking different from the thinking we've done earlier this week?

What types of things did you record?

Did any of the thinking you did help you understand the text better? Give an example.

Follow-Up

This lesson cycle is just the beginning of teaching students to record their thinking while reading. My goal in this cycle is for students to see the many ways they think while they read and to see some possibilities for recording thinking. I want them to see that this often supports their understanding. My work during this cycle is to observe for things to build on as the year goes on. Much of the follow-up work will be within other cycles of study, so the follow-up for the cycle is long term.

Minilesson Cycles Planner

Cycle Topic

What are the big goals I have for this study?

Which books might I use? Why? What types of things am I looking for in books for this cycle?

How will I provide for students to enter at their own level?

What will I be assessing? Does the assessment match the big picture goals?

CHAPTER 2

Exploring Characters: Breaking Down *the* Standards

When I think of the books that live inside me, it is almost always characters that come to mind first: Esperanza in The House on Mango Street, *Sethe in* Beloved, *Raskolnikov in* Crime and Punishment, *Scout in* To Kill a Mockingbird. *Every one of these characters has made the journey from trial to triumph. Teaching students how characterization works can be a key for unlocking comprehension as well as a door opening to a lifetime love affair with books.*

—Carol Jago

When I think about my own reading and my favorite books from different eras of my life, it is the characters that I remember. I remember Betsy, Nancy Drew, and Mary Lennox from my elementary years as a reader. Although I don't remember their names, I remember the four children locked in the attic of the Flowers in the Attic series—the books I read during my teen years. I remember Claude from *Body and Soul* by Frank Conroy. I remember the Morgans and the Langs in *Crossing to Safety* by Wallace Stegner. Although I can't recollect the details of most of these stories, these characters have stayed with me for many years.

If we want our students to discover fictional characters who change the way they see the world, they need to know many ways that they can talk and think about characters in books. No matter their age or level, they can think deeply about characters if we scaffold the conversations for them.

As Carol Jago says in *Crash! The Currency Crisis in American Culture: A Report from NCTE*, "Literature reflects the human condition. Reading about heroes like Janie Crawford and Huck Finn who must fend for themselves helps us put our own experiences into perspective and sometimes gives us the strength to carry on" (2009, 2).

I worry that too often we merely ask students to identify the main character or to create a web of character traits. Understanding characters and thinking deeply about the issues they face is far more important than being able to identify the main character in a book.

I know that conversations over the course of the year will build on one another. We never "finish" a character discussion. Instead, we are constantly adding to the ways in which we can talk, think, and write about characters. I choose books that give kids many ways into talking about characters.

There are many possible directions to go with a character cycle. Character development is something we learn about throughout our lives as readers. This lesson cycle is designed to help students see new ways to think about characters, with the curriculum in mind. My assessments showed that these students relied on describing characters in very simple ways (what they liked, what they looked like, and so on) and could benefit from new ways to think about character development.

It is not my intent to introduce all of the ways that readers learn about characters. Instead, I want students to become aware of the many ways that authors tell us about the characters in books, and to begin to practice talking about what they know about characters. I know this is the beginning of a lifelong conversation around ways to think about characters that will continue to grow.

Common Core Standard #3 Focuses In on Character
Vertically Aligned Grades 3–5

Grade 3	Grade 4	Grade 5
RL. 3.3 Describe characters in a story (e.g., their traits, motivations, or feelings) and how their actions contribute to the sequence of events.	RL. 4.3 Describe in depth a character, setting, or event in a story or drama, drawing on specific details in the text (e.g., characters' words, thoughts, or actions).	RL. 5.3 Compare and contrast two or more characters, settings, or events in a story or drama, drawing on specific details in the text (e.g., how characters interact).

Although the standards in the Common Core look similar across the grades when it comes to the concept of character, there is a lot of depth to each of the above statements. Digging in and unpacking how to help students reach these goals is key to planning. If we look at the goals for grades 3–5, we can see that we want students to be able to know characters well. This cycle is a first step in helping readers think beyond those literal things we know about characters.

In grade four, students are expected to "Describe in depth a character, setting, or event in a story or drama, drawing on *specific details in the text* (e.g., *characters' words, thoughts,* or *actions*)."

To plan well, I need to break this standard down for myself. For students to be able to meet this standard, they need to

- have many strategies for learning about characters,
- understand that describing a character in depth goes beyond regurgitating what the author tells us, and
- be able to support their thinking about a character with details from the text.

My next step is determining how to get to these three big goals.

The more a reader understands a character, the easier it is to connect to that character and to learn from his or her experiences. I want children to know that authors often give us a little information about a character at a time. It is our job as readers to integrate each new piece of information with what we've learned previously in the text. I want them to pay attention to the many ways in which we come to know characters. In this cycle, I also want to give students multiple ways to talk and think about the characters in the books they read.

I cannot expect students to pick up these specific skills on their own by doing lesson after lesson on how "readers find out about characters in a variety of ways." They won't compare characters (a goal in the Common Core) if they don't have lots of strategies for thinking about them. I have to break down the concepts so kids have specific strategies to use on their own. The Common Core says that students should compare two or more charachers. I have found that breaking this concept into smaller chunks helps. It is in the breaking down that the teaching happens.

For example, some goals I have for students over the course of this minilesson cycle are to understand the following:

- Authors help us get to know characters in a variety of ways.
- The more we know about a character, the better we can predict and understand his or her actions.
- Important characters often change over time.
- Understanding how characters see the world is critical to understanding their thoughts, relationships, and actions.
- There are *words* that readers use when they think and talk about characters in fiction. These words give us ways to think and talk at a deeper level.

Which Mentor Texts Might I Use?

I look for books that will introduce character analysis in ways that make the most sense for students in grades 3–5.

When I think about the books I introduce to kids during a character cycle, I am looking for characters who stay with students long after I read the book. Sometimes this is a gut feeling, but there are specific things I have come to look for when choosing books to use in a character study. I pay attention to the following things when gathering books in this cycle:

A **character's name in the title** such as *Stand Tall, Molly Lou Melon* by Patty Lovell. When a character's name is in the title of a book, this often tells me that the book is more character than plot based, and might be a good one for this cycle.

Several books that focus on the same character or characters such as the *Wild Boars* by Meg Rosoff and Sophie Blackall or *Chowder* by Peter Brown.

Books with two characters who are great friends or who are siblings, such as the Elephant and Piggie series by Mo Willems, *Bella & Bean* by Rebecca Kai Dotlich, or the Charlie and Lola series by Lauren Child. These often make for the best conversations about relationships.

Books that include **several short stories about the same character(s)** such as *The One and Only Marigold* by Florence Parry Heide and *Henry and Mudge* by Cynthia Rylant. We can learn a lot about the characters in books like this because we see them in various settings.

Characters the students love and talk about on their own such as Melanie Watt's Scaredy Squirrel or the Pigeon from Mo Willems's series. I find that I can get a lot of mileage from using books with characters students already know and love, so I often listen in to hear which characters pop up in their informal conversations.

Beginning the Cycle: First Conversations About Characters

I often begin a study on characters with some favorite ones from beginning picture books, since I prefer to revisit characters with whom students are familiar. I find characters who appear in more than one book and read several in one sitting. Max and Ruby in the series by Rosemary Wells, the Pigeon by Mo Willems, Llama Llama by Anna Dewdney, and Scaredy Squirrel by Melanie Watt are familiar to many young students. After reading one or two of these books together, I invite students to predict the actions of the characters in the newest books in the series. This helps them see that the better you know a character, the better able you are to predict their actions, and that this is key to further talk about characters.

If students are not familiar with any of these picture book characters, I may use a book like *The One and Only Marigold* by Florence Parry Heide. A very lovable character, Marigold, stars in four short stories in this book. I can use this book in the same ways I would use the picture books listed above. After reading two of the vignettes, I ask students to discuss the predictions they have for Marigold in the final two stories, based on what they already know about her. I am not looking for a "right" answer. Instead, I am hoping that students begin to use what they know about a character to make solid predictions.

Here are some questions I might ask after the reading:

What do we know about this character?

How do we know these things?

If we were to read another book about this character, what could we predict?

I move from these first conversations to more formal lessons that help students build many ways to talk and think about characters. Although I plan the cycle in a sequential way, I know that I need to be flexible. I listen to the conversations that we have as a class to determine which book or point makes sense for the next day's lesson. Because I have many books and plans ready to use, it is easy to choose the one that will naturally build on the talk from one day to the next. I try to make a connection from something a child says one day to the next day's conversation, so that the discussion naturally builds and extends our thinking as a group.

LESSON Talking and Thinking About Characters

One of the ways we understand characters is by their relationships with others. Much of what we know about characters comes from ways in which the character behaves. For students to read deeply, looking at characters and their relationships with others is critical.

Themes of friendship and relationships are universal. A story is very seldom told about a character in isolation.

Possible Anchor Text

Any book from the Elephant and Piggie Series by Mo Willems works well. My favorite to use at the beginning of this conversation is *Today I Will Fly*. In this book, the two characters' differences and the way they respond to each other tells us a lot about each one individually.

How I Teach It

I begin by reading aloud the book *Today I Will Fly*. After the reading, I ask students to think about the ways in which Piggie and Elephant talk and act toward each other. I list some of the student responses on a chart. After we have five or six things listed, we go back to each one and I ask students to think about what each response tells us about the character. When Elephant tells Piggie no, she will not fly, what does that tell us about Elephant? What does Piggie's response to Elephant tell us about Piggie? We continue through the list with this conversation, helping students see that each action might tell us something new about the character or reinforces something we already knew.

Questions I Might Ask to Start the Conversation

Thinking back to the fourth-grade standard on characters, I want my students to be able to "draw on specific details from the text." So, the "How do you know?" part of the question is crucial for each step of the lesson. I want this first lesson to help students practice finding details in the text to support their thinking about characters.

> How are Piggie and Elephant the same? How do you know?
> How are Piggie and Elephant different? How do you know?
> What do you know about Elephant from the way he talks to and treats Piggie?
> What do you know about Piggie from the way she talks to and treats Elephant?

Follow-Up

Use similar prompts to connect this conversation with previous conversations about predicting characters' actions. Ask students after reading this book, "What might you predict about Elephant and Piggie in another book in the series?"

LESSON **Predicting Characters' Actions**

Learning about characters is about understanding the things that motivate them, and the reasons for their behaviors. As Richard Allington writes in *What Really Matters for Struggling Readers*, "It is easier to predict how DW will respond after having read three *Arthur* books, which means you have read a lot about DW and her relationship with her brother. . . . After a half-dozen *Arthur* books it becomes even easier to answer the question: What would DW do?" (2001, 64).

Possible Anchor Text

For this lesson I use a new book from a series that students in the group are familiar with. This could be any picture book series where a single main character is central to the story. Fancy Nancy, Scaredy Squirrel, and Fly Guy are all good choices for this lesson.

How I Teach It

I begin by asking the class to look at the cover of a new book in a series. For example, I show them *Fancy Nancy: Splendiferous Christmas* by Jane O'Connor. Then I say, "Knowing what you do about Fancy Nancy from other books in this series, what do you think she might do in this book?" We chart or discuss the ideas that we have, often supporting our thinking with Nancy's behaviors in other books we've read. This conversation is not about having correct predictions. Rather, it is about thinking about the things that we know about a character and looking for patterns in behavior.

Questions I Might Ask to Start the Conversation

What do we know about Fancy Nancy? What are some things that she does in every single book?

Think about other books you've read about this character. What do you think you can count on happening in this new book?

Below is a list that one third-grade class came up with during this lesson.

She might put too many decorations on the tree.
She might have pink lights.
She might have pink decorations.

She might pick out her own clothes.

She might have a sparkly holiday outfit.

She might be seeing Santa.

She might use French words.

She might make up words.

She might ruin something.

Follow-Up

I might follow up this lesson with a similar one the next day that extends this to a two-column chart. The first column would list the predictions, and the second column would connect the prediction to the reason(s) why that prediction makes sense based on what we know about the character.

LESSON **Character Voice**

I want students to understand that the ways a character speaks (his attitude, her tone, the ways he put words together) all tell us about the character. We learn a lot about characters by the things they say and the ways in which they say them. Often in simple texts, the author tells us many things about characters. But as books become more sophisticated, readers need to infer things about them. One of the ways to do this is to pay attention to the things characters say and the ways in which they say them.

Possible Anchor Book

One of my favorite books to use to talk about this is *There's a Wolf at the Door* by Zoe B. Alley. In this book, the Big Bad Wolf stars in five of our favorite traditional tales (all told in graphic novel form). I particularly like to use the first story of the *Three Little Pigs*. Although students know the Three Little Pigs well from other versions of the story they may have read, the way that these pigs speak makes them different from the same characters in different versions of this story. It is easy to see how a character's voice often defines him or her.

Questions I Might Ask To Start the Conversation

What did you know about this character? What in the text helped you discover this?

What are the different ways in which authors tell us about
characters?

Is there something this character said that told you something
about him or her?

Follow-Up

I might use *The True Story of the 3 Little Pigs!* by Jon Scieszka to reinforce
this point in a future lesson. In this story, the wolf from the traditional
tale tells his version of what happened. The character's voice is important, so we compare and contrast that with the wolf's voice in the different stories.

LESSON How Characters Change

The important characters in a story often change over the course of
the book. Introducing the idea that characters change over time and
showing examples of the ways in which they change helps students
begin to notice these things in their own reading. Students in grades
3–6 are often so focused on plot that they don't notice the ways in
which a character changes from the beginning to the end of a story.
These changes may be central to the plot and theme.

Possible Anchor Text

Scaredy Squirrel by Melanie Watt is the story of a squirrel who is afraid
of nearly everything. He has a plan in place for every emergency, and
avoids unsafe situations at all costs. Although Scaredy Squirrel doesn't
change a great deal (he is still pretty worried at the end of the book),
he changes enough to begin a conversation about the ways in which
characters evolve. This is a fun book, with a character that kids like to
converse about.

How I Teach It

After reading aloud the first few pages of the book *Scaredy Squirrel,* I
ask students to think about all they know about Scaredy Squirrel. We
list those attributes on a chart that is big enough to refer to later. At the
middle of the book, I stop again and ask students to add to the things
they know about Scaredy Squirrel now. I also question if the attributes
we listed at the beginning are still accurate. At the end of the story, we

come back to our list and try to determine how Scaredy Squirrel has changed. I end the lesson by sharing with students that characters often change over the course of a story, and invite them to pay attention to other characters in their reading to see if they change.

Questions I Might Ask to Start the Conversation

How did Scaredy Squirrel change in the story?

Where in the story do you think he changed? Why?

What caused Scaredy Squirrel to change?

Can you think of characters in other books who change from the beginning to the end of the story?

Follow-Up

I might follow up with another book from the Scaredy Squirrel series. Scaredy Squirrel begins each book afraid of something, and he changes his thinking with a bit of experience. The evolution becomes a bit predictable, so for students who need a follow-up, I would introduce another book, read the first few pages, and allow them to predict ways in which Scaredy Squirrel might change in this new book. Characters often change in ways that resolve a problem, so this type of prediction will carry them far as readers.

LESSON Understanding a Character's Point of View

Knowing characters means understanding their point of view. Often, characters in books are different from us or from the people we know.

Possible Anchor Text

In *Willow* by Denise Brennan-Nelson and Rosemarie Brennan, Willow is a creative girl who drives her art teacher crazy with her unique ideas. But throughout the course of the story, Willow does not lose her spirit, keeping her upbeat and positive attitude. This is a character whose traits are obvious and accessible when talking about understanding the different ways in which a character sees the world.

How I Teach It

After reading this book aloud, I ask students to think about the things they know about Willow and the things they know about the art teacher. How does each see the world differently, and what in the book tells you that? We discuss or chart our thinking.

Questions I Might Ask to Start the Conversation

What do you know about this character by the way he or she acts?
How do you understand characters better when you know about their attitudes or perspectives?
Can you tell what kind of person this character is? How?

Follow-Up

For a follow-up to this lesson, I might use *Voices in the Park* by Anthony Browne. This is the story of a trip to the park, told by four different people. Each character tells his or her story of the trip, and it is clear that each has a slightly different perspective. This book can be used to help students see that you can infer a character's perspectives and motivations by listening to their words and paying attention to their actions.

LESSON Literary Language for Exploring Characters

Near the end of this cycle, I think it is important to introduce some common words used when talking about characters. I started to do this years ago when my fifth graders were talking about characters but without any understanding of their role in the story. I suspected that literary language would help them think more deeply about the characters in the book. Terms like *protagonist, antagonist, dynamic character,* and *static character* give kids in grades 3–6 new ways to think about characters. Even though the Common Core does not require these words until middle school and high school, I have found it is important to introduce them before then.

I am not concerned whether elementary school students know specific literary vocabulary, and I worry when kids are tested on this type of vocabulary at that level. My purpose in introducing literary terms to elementary students is to help them see the various ways in which we can think about characters. When students try to decide if a character is dynamic or static, they are really looking for evidence to see if and how that character has changed over time. The better they can understand a character, the more deeply they can understand the entire text.

It is helpful for students to encounter these words informally and in oral language before they become part of the required curriculum. I want them to be familiar with these words for the next phase of their learning.

Possible Anchor Text

For this lesson, I pull many of the texts that we've used during the course of this cycle. Revisiting the books and thinking about these terms as they relate to characters we've been discussing is an easy way to introduce these words and ways of thinking.

How I Teach It

To start these conversations, I usually post the terms *protagonist, antagonist, static character,* and *dynamic character* and others along with their definitions on a board in the room where everyone can see them. Then I return to many of the books we've read throughout the cycle and we talk about the different characters in each one. We might revisit Fancy Nancy and talk about protagonists as well as static and dynamic characters. We might go back to *The Three Little Pigs* and talk about the antagonist. Traditional fairy tales and children's movies are great anchors for this talk. *Cinderella* and *Goldilocks and the Three Bears* are great ways to begin this conversation.

Follow-Up

After we've introduced the words and brought them to the conversation, I leave the words posted and let kids know that readers often use them when they talk about characters and that they might want to use them in future conversations. Usually, after a few days of not being quite sure how to use them, the kids find ways to bring them into the talk around books.

Next Steps

After having about five to seven minilessons using picture books, I want to make sure that students can begin to transfer this thinking about characters to their independent reading. The ways that we think about characters are similar, whether we are talking about Max and

Ruby or Harry Potter. After several days of introducing picture books and ways in which readers think about characters, I'll plan a few lessons to help transfer that thinking to longer books and other media. During minilessons, informal conversations, and reading conferences, I may ask one of the following questions to help students make this transfer:

> What are you learning about the character in your book? What questions do you still have?
>
> Has the character in your book said or done anything that helps you know him or her better? Tell us about that.
>
> Who do you think the protagonist is in the book you are reading? What makes you think so?
>
> Is anyone reading a book in which the character is changing? Tell us about that.

Booklist: Books That Support Talk About Characters

Since this is a quick cycle, I know that for the conversation to continue, we will have to revisit these ideas throughout the year. Here are additional books I use when I want to extend the cycle about characters.

Books with Two Distinct Characters

The Pain and the Great One by Judy Blume

> Judy Blume's classic picture book *The Pain and the Great One* has been expanded to a chapter book series for older readers. By following the siblings (older sister/younger brother), you get to see both points of view through several family events. Using the picture book and these short chapter books together invites lots of dialogue about the views of each member of a family, and what sometimes causes conflict between siblings.

Bella & Bean by Rebecca Kai Dotlich

> This is one of my favorite stories of friendship and the kinds of conflicts good friends have. We learn about both characters mostly through their interactions with each other.

Wilfrid Gordon McDonald Partridge by Mem Fox

This is the story of Wilfrid Gordon McDonald Partridge and the way he tries to help Miss Nancy find her memory. We are told some things about Wilfrid in the early pages of the book, but we learn more about him through his relationships with the people at the retirement home.

Characters Who Change Over Time

The Summer My Father Was Ten by Pat Brisson

The main character in this story has to mend the relationship he has with a neighbor after destroying his garden while playing with friends. Both the boy and the neighbor change their behaviors over the course of the book.

Emma's Rug by Allen Say

This is a very sophisticated picture book that I like to use after we have already talked extensively about characters. Emma is a young artist who relies on her rug to get her ideas. In this story, Emma changes in the way she thinks about her art and sees herself.

Perspectives in Learning About Character

Why Do I Have to Eat Off the Floor? by Chris Hornsey

In the book, the dog asks its owner many questions such as the one that serves as the title. My favorite is "Why can't I drive the car?" The dog is a typical house pet with some great facial expressions. Thinking about the dog's perspective—the things he might say if he could talk—is quite fun!

Arnie, the Doughnut by Laurie Keller

Have you ever thought about what it might feel like to be a doughnut that is about to be eaten? In this story, Laurie Keller shares the story of Arnie, a doughnut who is purchased by Mr. Bing. When Mr. Bing tries to eat Arnie, there are problems. It's an intriguing and humorous way to look at perspective.

Who Is Melvin Bubble? by Nick Bruel

In this book, the reader asks different characters about Melvin Bubble. Based on their relationship with Melvin, each

person gives us different insights about him. There is lots of
humor throughout the book, and it is fun to hear different
stories about Melvin from his father, mother, dog, and
others.

Dear Mother, Dear Daughter by Jane Yolen and Heidi Stemple
In this book, we hear several poetic conversations between a
mother and her daughter. The conversations deal with issues
like doing homework, cleaning your room, and other
common sources of tension between parents and children.
The mother and daughter respond to each other, and learn
to understand each other's perspectives.

Character's Voice

Wild Boars Cook and *Meet Wild Boars* by Meg Rosoff
These are two other fun books to continue conversations
about characters. Although the four wild boars are similar to
one another, each has a unique voice. Doris is one character
whose dialogue tells a great deal about who she is.

The Trucktown Series by Jon Scieszka
This newer series is an interesting one to use in discussions.
Although each of the characters is a truck, they all have
unique personalities. You come to expect certain things from
each truck character because of his or her distinctive voice.

Chester by Melanie Watt
Chester, the author's cat, is trying to take over as author of
the story Melanie Watt is writing. He uses a fat red marker to
rewrite each page the way he would like things to go. *Chester*
and the sequel *Chester's Back!* both have the same tension
between the way the author would like to see the story move
forward and the way Chester wants it to proceed.

CHAPTER 3

Teaching Theme:
It's All About
the Right Books

Elementary students can understand the concept of themes, but we're

often in such a hurry to move on to the next book or the next objective,

that we don't have time for hindsight—thinking about a book after we

read it.

—Aimee Buckner, *Teaching Themes Through Keywords*

When I work with teachers, theme seems to be one of the most difficult concepts for us to make accessible to elementary students. Many of us learned about theme while reading the classics in high school and college English classes, yet we still don't have a firm handle on it.

Theme is not an easy word to define. In her book *Classics in the Classroom*, Carol Jago defines it as "the central meaning or idea of a literary work" (2004, 71). As teachers, we need to understand theme deeply enough to teach it in a way that makes sense to young readers. Theme is about thinking beyond the plot of the story and exploring bigger messages. The middle elementary grades seem to be the perfect place to dig into this concept. There is no right answer for the theme of a story, as long as readers can support their thinking with evidence from the text. Several years ago my friend Mary Lee Hahn and I were both reading the same adult novel, *The Dogs of Babel* by Carolyn Parkhurst. As we talked about the book later, you would have thought we had read totally different stories. Mary Lee talked about the dog, and I talked about the relationship of the couple. We both understood the plot, but we were hooked on different themes.

I've had to really think about what makes sense for kids—my goal can no longer be about students finding the right theme. Instead, I want students to know how authors write and leave clues about what they are saying. I want to break it down for them so that they have the strategies to discover theme on their own.

My journey with teaching theme has been a powerful one. What I have learned over and over again since I have let go of a "one right theme" idea is that my students often discover themes that are much more in depth and true to the story than those that I have discovered or that show up in the teacher guides. Many anthologies and tests "dumb down" theme for kids, but our students are able to discover and understand extremely powerful themes if given the tools to do so.

Over the years, I have noticed that the third and fourth graders I work with have the skills of predicting, retelling, and questioning. They are very focused on plot through the primary grades. This makes good sense, since most of the books they read in the early years are focused on plot. When I take a hard look at the types of picture books and early chapter books young children love, most are story-driven. Theme is a natural next-step concept for readers to explore.

Theme shows up in the standards at various times throughout the K–12 language arts program. In the Common Core, theme is introduced in grade three and builds from there. Third grade is probably the first time students begin to think deeply about theme.

I think first about the big picture of theme. In a theme cycle, my big goal is for students to understand that they have the skills to determine the theme—they don't have to wait for someone else to tell them the theme of a text. Big concepts for this cycle include the following:

• Readers have the power to determine the theme in a text.*

- Authors often write a story with a bigger message about life to the reader.
- There is often more than one theme in a book.
- There are universal themes that appear often in books.
- A theme works across an entire text.

* This is the umbrella understanding that I cannot sacrifice throughout this cycle. The bullets below this umbrella concept are ways to help students achieve it.

Scaffolding Learning Through Book Choice: A Menu of Resources

When I am choosing my resources, I need to remind myself that I want to teach the reader, not the book. I want to find books that give my students practice using the strategies I give them for finding themes, make themes accessible for students, and help them see themes clearly. After these first few books, I move to texts that require a bit more thinking and problem solving.

When I do my big-picture planning, I am creating a general menu for myself. I select a set of books I plan to use in minilessons, but I also want several extras that I can use once I see where each lesson goes. Until I begin the unit, I cannot be certain how students will respond to each lesson, so I pull together a menu of books and lessons that I hope will scaffold the concept for kids. My menu includes books that I will use throughout the cycle and that provide various levels of support, depending on how students respond to each lesson.

If I want to empower students to find themes on their own, I need my teaching to focus on that, rather than repeating a theme that I've identified.

Rethinking the Ways We Choose Books for Minilessons

When I think about theme units of the past, I am reminded of the units of the 1980s when we as teachers chose six to eight books with a survival theme and allowed kids to choose one to read. Although these units immersed kids in a universal theme, it was the teachers rather than the students who did the work of finding that theme.

We need to rethink these theme units for a variety of reasons. First of all, the theme was chosen before the unit began. Students were never given the message that readers could identify themes through reading. Second, although the books often spanned reading levels, most books in a thematic unit were novels that took a great deal of time to read. I would rather my students practice reading for different themes in several short texts over a two-week period.

We often use books in our teaching because we love them. There is nothing wrong with that for many reading goals. But for explicit minilesson work, I need books that offer far more than merely being personal favorites or great stories. Each text needs to provide something explicit to the students I teach.

I think carefully about accessibility for my students. In the past I chose books for my students that I loved as an adult but that kids could access only at a minimal level because the ideas or concepts were too grown up. I shared books that were over my students' heads. I stuck with the same tried-and-true books that I'd used for years. Even though these classics are great stories, they no longer provide a picture of the world today. If I want students to read with a sense of depth, I want the story to be relevant for children in their world today.

We also make mistakes in book choice by relying on books selected by other professionals. Book lists are everywhere, and I have definitely been guilty of using books recommended by professionals without thinking about what makes sense for my kids. I would check them out at the library and begin using them immediately. Lists created by other educators are definitely helpful (in fact, I am providing some in this book!), but we can't blindly use the books suggested. They provide a good starting place, but the experiences we have with books and our students are the ultimate criteria for choosing the right book for a minilesson. Now when I use books recommended by others, I do a lot of research first. I spend time reading each book to see how it might build on what my students already know. I try to know each book as well as the person who recommended it to me. Sometimes the books don't work because my students have different life or reading experiences. Sometimes I find that the book is a perfect fit for my teaching. Other times, I find the opposite.

This is also true for books I have used in the past. A book that worked for one class may not work for another. I have seen lessons go poorly because the book didn't provide the scaffold it did for a previous class. When a book doesn't provide the right scaffold, I end up "telling" for most of the lesson. This goes against my biggest goal of the cycle—empowering readers to determine theme.

Accessibility to children is the most important factor in choosing a book. For me accessibility is the idea that kids can think through the work of the minilesson with very little help from me. I have too many memories of me, as the teacher, doing the work of thinking because the concept in a book is well beyond a child's reach. I try to find books that make the concept I am teaching very clear to students—in a way that they can discover on their own. It is often difficult to find books that support students in practicing their thinking while providing enough support for students to solve problems on their own.

"Shopping" for Books

In order to match books specifically to the things I want students to notice, I can't wait until a few days or even a few weeks before I begin my teaching cycle. Instead, I am always on the lookout for new texts with specific elements. I have learned to shop for books in bookstores and libraries more strategically and with intention.

One of the things that I learned in my years as a school librarian is that some books invite a certain response from readers. Because I have had the chance to read books over and over to different groups of students, I can predict how students will respond to certain pages, words, and illustrations. Well-written books are teachers in themselves. If the author knows the age of the reader he or she writes for, the text and themes are accessible, and students respond with depth and independence.

I shop for minilesson books a bit differently these days. I have in my head the things I have to teach across the year. I used to have content ideas in my head, and was always on the lookout for nonfiction books about Ohio history or electricity. Although I still look for those topic-specific books, I have found that those are easier to discover. It takes less digging to find the perfect book to extend or enrich a content unit.

But to teach concepts such as theme, character analysis, and inferring, the book must be one that invites the reader to participate in the discovery. For the first cycle on theme, I want the books that really break down the idea of theme for them by introducing certain elements. For example, if I want the focus of my lesson to be the idea that readers can support their thinking with evidence, I will choose a wordless book such as Jeannie Baker's *Window*, in which the illustrations can be used to understand the theme. With each book, I hope to add to students' understanding in a strategic way. Individually, each book has one feature that stands out. Collectively, the pile of books I choose will help build understanding over time.

I also want books that "level the playing field." I want there to be an "in" for students who struggle with reading, so they can understand the bigger concepts of theme. I choose books that have visual as well as text support.

Finding the Perfect Books for Teaching Theme

I want students to know how to find theme in any fiction they are reading. I want them to be aware of the critical devices authors use to tell their story and to give their message. I have found that if I break this down for students, they can begin to formulate a list of several things to look for after a short cycle on theme. My goal is for them to be able to transfer each of these things to any text they read in the future, as they are all very universal.

Readers can think about theme by

- considering the author's message throughout the entire book,
- paying close attention to those things that come up over and over in a text,
- knowing that universal themes come up over and over again,
- understanding how various storylines fit together,
- thinking about the way in which the problem in the plot is solved,
- thinking about metaphors and symbols that the author uses, and
- supporting thinking about theme with evidence in the text.

I look for books that will help me meet these goals. I look for books with:

a very obvious theme
two storylines that come together in some way
repeated language
illustrations that are key to theme
similar themes
a dedication or beginning quote that gives the book new meaning

I also keep my eye out for books with complex themes. Although I don't want to use these more complex books early in the cycle, these books become my goal—what I hope kids can make sense of on their own at the end of the cycle. Books such as *Voices in the Park* by Anthony Browne and *The Goblin and the Empty Chair* by Mem Fox are texts with a complexity I would save for the end of a cycle.

Each book and lesson in this theme cycle allows students to discover the ways in which authors lead us to themes. I want my students to have a variety of ways to dig into a book. I know that not every one of these strategies will work for every book, and I want my students to know that too. Authors tell stories in various ways. It will be up to the reader to determine which of these strategies helps them as they read.

Before I begin, I think about the logical sequence for these lessons. I want them to build on one another, to layer on more complexity as we go.

Keeping an End in Mind

Depending on the specific grade level I teach, and the standards I am expected to meet, these are starting points. I may spend two or three days on one idea if it seems difficult for students. I may back up if I see what I've done is too far of a reach for kids. I may go forward if I notice that kids are grasping ideas about theme more quickly than I had expected.

I find that when I am very intentional and break down the concepts I am teaching, finding books becomes easy. When I know I am looking for epigraphs, I can go through my library to find those books with epigraphs. There is nothing magical about the books on my list, except that they are the ones that are working for me right now. There are many others that would fit the same needs.

In the end, I don't want kids to be able to spit out the theme that I identify for the book. Instead, I want them to know how to use the clues in the text to determine theme on their own. I want to teach them strategies to empower them to find the theme in anything that they read. If I keep that end in mind, choosing books is much easier.

LESSON **Plot Versus Theme**

Even if students can tell us the theme of a book, they often get confused by the academic vocabulary of literature. If we want them to be able to participate in conversations about theme, the language is important. When students can see the difference between plot and theme, they can begin to look at how authors use plot to give the reader a message.

Possible Anchor Text

I like to use a wordless picture book for this lesson. These books allow students to tell the story (retelling plot) in their own words and then to talk about plot versus theme. A book that works well because of the easy sequence of events is *A Circle of Friends* by Giora Carmi. For lessons like this one, I look for books that have a clear, sequential plot—one that is simple to retell. I don't want us to spend much time retelling the story since that is not the goal of this lesson.

How I Teach It

We usually begin this lesson by reading the book *A Circle of Friends*. Because this is a wordless picture book, I share it silently so students will experience it first on their own. Then I ask, "If you were going to put words to this story, how would the story go?" On a chart, we retell the story with words, making sure we have a beginning, middle, and end, and that we capture the important events. I then write "Plot" at the top of this chart paper. I tell the class that what happens in a story is called the plot. But, I tell them, readers read beyond plot. Often in stories, there is a bigger message or theme that the author is trying to tell us through the story, and theme is different from plot. A theme is the big message of the story. I refer to the chart and reread it to them.

I remind them that these are the things that happened in the story but that the author had a big message for us through the story that is called the theme. I ask kids what they thought the theme or message might be, and I write those on another chart paper with the heading of "Theme."

At this point, I am not worried about whether students completely understand what theme is or whether their theme predictions are correct. I am just going for the idea that there is a difference between plot (what happens) and theme (big message). I am not looking for mastery, as we will be revisiting this idea throughout the cycle. This lesson helps set the stage for those ongoing conversations.

Questions I Might Ask to Start the Conversation

What is the story about? If you were going to tell someone what happened at the beginning, middle, and end, what would you say?

How did you decide what was important enough for the retelling of the plot?

When you think about theme, what do you think the author might be trying to tell us? Why do you think that?

Follow-Up

I sometimes introduce this idea with short movie clips instead of a book. I want my students to see that stories are told in many ways and that no matter how they are told, they have many of the same elements.

Continuing to add the word *plot* to any work with retelling or summary will be important for helping kids see the difference between plot and theme.

I might also include a wall of words we use when we talk about plot and words when we talk about theme. For example, *and then* would go on the plot chart. So would *first*. This chart would be for them to refer to, and to add to throughout the cycle.

LESSON **Stated Versus Implied Themes**

Almost all themes are implied. Very seldom will authors come out and tell us the message they are trying to convey through their story. However, reading between the lines is often new for readers in grades

3–6. They naturally read for plot until now, and are not accustomed to reading beyond the literal meaning of text. I find it is good to start with a sample of a stated theme.

Possible Anchor Text

One of my favorite books for a lesson like this is *Pete the Cat: I Love My White Shoes* by Eric Litwin. This is a book that is a song, and the end of the book states the moral or theme of the book. I also like to use books that have obvious themes for this lesson. Books such as *The Little Engine That Could* by Watty Piper and Loren Long have clear themes for upper elementary students.

How I Teach It

Reading (or watching via YouTube) the book *Pete the Cat: I Love My White Shoes* by Eric Litwin is a great way to begin this lesson. Kids of all ages love this book, especially when it is shared as a song. At the end of the book, the author tells us the moral of this story. This provides the perfect opportunity to talk about how themes are or are not like morals, and how this theme is an easy one to decipher because the author tells us what it is. After this discussion, I read *The Little Engine That Could* and discuss with students that most books have implied themes—themes that the author does not come right out and say. I share the book, asking if anyone has heard this or another version of the story. We then talk about the implied theme, and what information from the text gives clues about the theme.

Questions I Might Ask to Start the Conversation

Yesterday, we talked about theme versus plot. Do you remember what a theme is?

Eric Litwin tells us the theme in *Pete the Cat*. Can you think of other stories in which the author tells readers the theme?

Usually a theme is implied. Can you think of other books we've read in which the theme is implied but you could figure it out?

Follow-Up

If necessary, I might use other classic titles with very obvious themes to continue to think about the idea of theme. Books such as *The Great Big Enormous Turnip* by Alexei Tolstoy have accessible themes. I might share a few of these well-known stories to solidify the idea of implied theme.

LESSON **When Two Storylines Come Together**

As students begin to read more sophisticated texts in the elementary grades, they often come across books with more than one storyline. Experienced readers know that these storylines are somehow connected and will eventually come together in some way. But many intermediate grade readers have never experienced this type of story. In terms of theme, there is often a point in the story when two storylines come together, and this point is sometimes critical to the overall theme of the book. Something usually changes at that point that readers need to pay attention to.

Possible Anchor Text

Artie and Julie by Chin-Yuan Chen is my favorite book for teaching this idea of two connected stories. This is the story of two characters, a rabbit and a lion, who become friends against the odds. The story is told in two parts, and the pages are actually cut into two pieces so that the storylines are truly and tangibly separate. When the two characters meet, the pages are no longer cut and the story becomes one. This is the best book I have seen for presenting two storylines coming together in a concrete way.

How I Teach It

We begin this lesson by talking about books that seem to have more than one story going on at the same time. Students may have experience with books by Jan Brett such as *The Gingerbread Baby* or *The Mitten* in which an added layer of the story is happening in the border illustrations. I share with students that as they continue to grow as readers, they might come across books that have two stories happening at the same time that don't seem to be related to each other. I might share a few books that I've read or texts in the classroom library that do this. *The Wanderer* by Sharon Creech and *A Long Walk to Water* by Linda Sue Park come to mind. I let them know that when this happens in fiction, the stories often come together and become one story at some point, or the stories will obviously connect in some way. When that happens to me as a reader I know to pay attention, because the theme is becoming more clear. Then I introduce and read *Artie and Julie*. After the reading, we talk about the two storylines, and then revisit the page where the stories first come together and become one. At this point, we speculate on the theme of the book and the reasons for our predictions. I am not worried about the themes that they come up with. This is just practice for understanding theme in general (since I introduced the concept only a few days ago.

Questions I Might Ask to Start the Conversation

Can you think of any books that have two stories going on at the same time?

With this question, kids may respond with books like Henry and Mudge in which the "chapters" are each stand-alone stories. This is okay, because we can then talk about the difference between stories happening at different times and stories happening at the same time.

Before we get too far into the book *Artie and Julie*, I'll stop and ask how they think the two stories might come together. I want them to read while anticipating that the two stories will be coming together and predicting how they might.

I'd prompt them by saying, "Let's look back at the page where the stories come together. Why is this an important part of the story? What is the author trying to tell us? Why do you think that?"

Follow-Up

If students don't readily understand this idea, I might revisit books by Jan Brett such as *The Mitten* or *The Gingerbread Baby* and have students look carefully at the story the text tells and the story the border illustrations reveal. We would have similar conversations about the point where the stories come together.

I would also invite kids to think about television shows that they watch where two or more storylines are going on at a time.

LESSON　Repeated Language in a Story

Authors use certain words, phrases, symbols, and metaphors in their writing. Their repeated use indicates that the author places importance on these words. No matter how complex the text, it's important for readers to pay attention to things that come up more than once.

Possible Anchor Text

Picture books often have obvious repeated phrases. A book written for young children with a verse that is repeated throughout gives kids a tangible way to remember that repeated words and phrases are important. A book that I like to use for this lesson is *Whoever You Are* by Mem Fox. The repeated phrase in this book reminds readers that whoever you are, we are all more the same than we are different. The repeated phrase occurs every few pages or so—almost like the refrain in a song.

How I Teach It

I often start this lesson by reading the book aloud, prefacing the read by asking the students to listen to the words that the author uses over and over. After the reading, we revisit that book and talk about the things we notice about the phrase. I sometimes enlarge the repeated phrase for the entire class to see.

We talk about the importance of words and phrases that come up over and over again throughout a story. We discuss how words and phrases are often a clue from the author about the theme of the book.

Questions I Might Ask to Start the Conversation

What is the repeated phrase telling readers? What makes you think that?

Do you notice anything about the placement of the repeated phrase? How do you think Mem Fox decided on where to put the phrase?

What is so important about these words that Mem Fox uses them over and over throughout the book?

Follow-Up

As a follow-up to this lesson, I might ask students to pay attention to reading, movies, songs, television commercials, and so on over the next several days to see if they notice repeated phrases in other media. Spending time talking about repeated words and phrases will help them listen intentionally beyond the classroom.

I might also do a quick lesson on the fact that the words in the repeated phrase of *Whoever You Are* also show up in the title of the book. I would ask students pay close attention as a reader to times that the author uses words from the title in the text, since this is another clue about the theme.

LESSON **Universal Themes**

Whether we are watching a movie or reading a book, no matter where we are in the world, there are universal themes that come up over and over in stories. Themes such as friendship, grief, and collaboration are often explored. When kids understand that there are big themes that go across age, culture, and media, they begin to look for these universal themes. The themes become a starting place to think about a more specific theme.

I want students to know that a one-word theme, although a great beginning, is not enough. More thinking and deep reading can help students get to more specific messages within that big idea.

Possible Anchor Text

Wanda's Roses by Pat Brisson is a book about a little girl who wants to turn a vacant city lot into a beautiful garden. Although it seems impossible, she has lots of people to help her out, and not in the way you'd expect. I'd pair this book with another like *Pumpkin Soup* by Helen Cooper in which the characters work together to create a delicious soup. Although these are different stories, one of the main themes in both is the importance of people working together. There are many other books that share this universal theme.

How I Teach It

I start out by introducing the idea of universal themes to students, letting them know that there are some themes that they will come across over and over and over again. I often share examples from my own reading to start this conversation. I talk to them about the fact that even though the theme is common, each author or story may be saying something a little bit different about it. I'd let them know that we are about to read two quick stories that have similar themes.

I begin by reading *Wanda's Roses*, as it has several themes within the story. After the reading, we make a chart of the possible themes in the book. Then I read *Pumpkin Soup*. After the reading of *Pumpkin Soup*, we look at the chart of themes in *Wanda's Roses* and see if any are similar.

Usually the children quickly discover working together as a common theme, although there may be others too. We then discuss whether the authors are saying the exact same thing about working together or have a unique take on the theme.

Questions I Might Ask to Start the Conversation

What is similar about what these two authors are telling us?
What is different?
What is the big idea of each of these books? What is a more specific theme?
How does talking about the big idea or theme help you start thinking about the more specific theme?
What are some other books that you've read that have a theme of working together?

Follow-Up

I follow up with collections of short stories such as *Lost and Found: Three Dog Stories* by Jim LaMarche or poetry anthologies such as *Moving Day* by Ralph Fletcher. Looking across pieces that an author chooses to put together helps readers think about these universal themes in a new way. The title *Lost and Found* is a clue about the theme of the book. The stories each give the message in a different way. In *Moving Day* and other poetry anthologies, the poems work together to create a unified message. Although each individual piece may have a theme, the whole book also has a theme. I might also try to tie in short videos to show how theme transcends medium.

LESSON Metaphors and Symbols as a Way Into Theme

For our students to learn to read between the lines of literature, they need to know what is possible. Often authors use symbols and metaphors in their writing to convey a deeper message. I want my students to know that authors often write about one thing but are really talking about something else.

Possible Anchor Text

Gift books seem to work well for this lesson. There are many books that are written to celebrate graduation, and these work well to introduce students to the idea of metaphors in writing as a way into theme. I look for books in which the metaphor is very accessible to young readers. I use the terms *metaphor* and *symbol* very loosely in this lesson, as the concept I am trying to introduce is a difficult one.

How I Teach It

I begin this lesson by reading aloud *Walk On!* by Marla Frazee. This is a book that on the surface seems like a book about a baby learning to walk, but it is much more than that. I don't say anything before the reading, except that I have a great book to share. I read this brief book aloud, and we talk about it. After the short discussion, I turn to the dedication page, where the author tells us she wrote the book to her son Graham as he was preparing to go to college. This immediately changes the meaning of the book. Then I ask students what the author is *really* saying. We look at each page and read each line, now that we know that the true meaning of the text is not really about learning to walk. This book makes it easy for students to think about each line, what it says literally, and what it might mean.

I often follow up with the book *Mrs. Spitzer's Garden* by Edith Pattou, which is about a teacher who grows a garden. The garden is a metaphor for the classroom, and the author uses several other metaphors throughout. This book is a little less accessible to students, so I would not present it first. However, gardens and growing show up so often as symbols in literature that I would move to this after students were successful with *Walk On!*

Questions I Might Ask to Start the Conversation

What is the book *Walk On!* by Marla Frazee about?

Now that we've read the dedication, what do you think *Walk On!* is about?

Thinking about the dedication, what does each of the pages tell her son?

What is the author telling us in this story?

What is the story *Mrs. Spitzer's Garden* about? Do you think the author is really talking about gardening in this book? Why or why not?

Follow-Up

City Dog, Country Frog by Mo Willems is a book I might use as a follow-up or extension of this lesson. There are many opportunities to discuss the symbols of the seasons or the "froggy smile" in the illustrations in this book, leading to larger discussions of theme.

LESSON Analyzing Solutions to Understand Themes

The way in which a problem is solved is often one of the keys to determining the theme of a text. I find that in the primary grades, students have a great deal of experience talking about problems and solutions in stories. They often come to the upper elementary grades with confidence about analyzing problems and solutions that can be used to move them forward as readers. Helping students use the things they know about plot to identify themes builds deeper reading habits.

Possible Anchor Text

For a lesson like this one, I want a book that has a clear problem and solution. I want the solution to be obvious, so that the conversation can be about the theme. A few books that work well for a lesson like this (clear problem/solution and accessible theme) are *Lilly's Purple Plastic Purse* by Kevin Henkes, *The Summer My Father Was Ten* by Pat Brisson, and *Wanda's Roses*, also by Pat Brisson. *Emma's Rug* by Allen Say is also a terrific book for this lesson, but because it is a much more sophisticated solution, I'd use it later in our conversation.

How I Teach It

I read aloud *Lilly's Purple Plastic Purse* and ask students to identify the problem (Lilly acts out in class and gets mad at her teacher) and solution (Lilly realizes she was wrong and writes a note and makes cookies for her teacher). I then tell students that sometimes the solution is a clue for the main theme. If you think hard and analyze the way in which the problem is solved, I say, you can figure out what the author is trying to tell you. Think about what the solution in this book is telling us.

I then give students time to turn and talk so that they can process their thinking around the solution. Then we chart our ideas as a class and discuss the theme of the book.

Questions I Might Ask to Start the Conversation

What was the most important thing about the way Lilly solved
the problem?

What did Lilly have to learn to solve her problem?

Were there other ways that Lilly could have solved the problem
that would have changed the theme of the story?

How did Lilly change because of the problem/solution?

Follow-Up

Depending on the level of understanding students have about this concept, I might do a similar lesson with the other books. If students don't
seem to need more practice with the idea, I'd try to transfer it to more
complex texts. Using our read-aloud or a book we'd read together in
the past, I'd start a three-column chart with the headings "Problem,"
"Solution," and "Theme." For each of the books we'd read, we could
list the problem and solution and then discuss what those implications
would be for theme. This would help students see how to transfer the
same kinds of thinking to longer, more sophisticated texts.

LESSON One-Word Ideas Versus Specific Themes

It is often easy for young readers to get the general idea of a story, but
it may take rereading to determine the specific message. This lesson is
designed to help students expand their thinking and get to a deeper
understanding of theme.

I want my students to go beyond one-word answers when it comes
to theme. Often in the primary grades, students begin to identify big
ideas such as friendship, loss, and cooperation as simple themes from
a book. But in the intermediate grades, it is important for students to
go beyond one-word ideas and understand more sophisticated and specific themes from the author.

Possible Anchor Text

South by Patrick McDonnell is a wordless picture book that works well
for this lesson. I like to use this book because it is clearly about friendship, but the reader needs to dig a little deeper to determine what the

author might be telling us about that theme. Books with friendship themes are great for this lesson because students tend to understand a lot about issues of friendship from their own experiences.

How I Teach It

I've picked up several copies of this book because it is such a good one to use for lots of minilessons. But the lesson is just as doable by projecting the book onto a screen to discuss the theme. To teach this lesson, I share the book with students so that all can see the pictures. For the first reading, we just look at the pictures silently and don't do much discussing. After the first read, I ask students to give me a one-word thought about what the theme might be. Common responses are friendship, love, and loss. If friendship is one of the choices, I usually choose to focus the conversation there, as it seems to be the one that causes the most conversation and critical thinking.

With friendship as the focus, we go back through the book, analyzing each page for what the story is saying about friendship. As we turn the pages, we chart each idea.

Finally, we look at the chart to infer a theme across the book based on our notes.

Questions I Might Ask to Start the Conversation

How can thinking about one word help us start to expand our ideas about theme?

How is a one-word theme different from a specific theme?

What are all the messages about friendship this book could be giving?

How do you think readers determine the theme when there are so many possibilities?

Follow-Up

This lesson supports the idea of universal themes and is a good way to scaffold understanding theme. For a follow-up to this lesson, I would find a book that focuses on a totally different theme, such as *Plant a Kiss* by Amy Krouse Rosenthal or *King Hugo's Huge Ego* by Chris Van Dusen. These books have themes other than friendship, so the lesson can be repeated with a new word and new thinking around the word.

LESSON **Theme Throughout a Text**

Students are usually able to identify things in a story that "teach us something." But they often look at specific scenes in the book rather than across an entire piece. Although a book may have many themes, the main themes need to span the entire book. There need to be episodes and events that lead the reader to the theme and that connect to each other.

Possible Anchor Text

Voices in the Park by Anthony Browne is a great book to use for this lesson. The book is told in four parts, each from a different character's perspective. This book is complex, and I would not use it early in the cycle on theme. However, once students can think in sophisticated ways about theme, this is a great book to stretch thinking. Because the book is told in four parts, it is obvious that the idea of theme is something that connects all parts of the text.

How I Teach It

After reading the book aloud to students, we go back to each section and talk about what message each section alone gives us. I remind them that a book may have many themes, but a main theme usually builds across an entire text. There are often many places where you can see the theme building, and the smaller pieces often add up to a bigger theme. Then I ask students to think about the ways in which the four stories work together. From there, we can infer some possible themes that work across the entire text, connecting the four parts.

Questions I Might Ask to Start the Conversation

Why did the author write this book as four separate stories?

Even though each separate story/part may have a message, how can we think about the message that works for each of these stories—both apart and together?

Why do you think the author chose to break this book into four parts? How does that structure support a larger theme?

How can you go about thinking across a whole story when thinking about theme, rather than on focusing on a specific part?

Follow-Up

For a follow-up to this lesson, I would revisit a book that we'd discussed previously. We'd quickly revisit the book and remind ourselves of the themes we inferred. Then we'd go page by page and think about the way that each scene or page builds to the overall theme. This allows students to see that the same thinking strategies can be used in books that are not as clearly divided as *Voices in the Park*.

CHAPTER 4

Nonfiction Reading: Rethinking Lesson Cycles We've Always Taught

The best-laid plans do not ever go quite as expected. Any lesson cycle, whether planned by a company, the school district, or an individual teacher, needs to have the flexibility to change as student needs shift.

One big factor in implementing cycles of study is an understanding that no cycle stands alone, and it is critical to take into account what students bring to a unit—what is already in place. Asking teachers to follow a pacing guide makes sense in theory, but not for teachers who plan based on student needs and responses. I have never experienced a lesson or unit that goes exactly according to my plans.

As teachers we all have our favorite units of study, and for good reason. Those of us who have taught a long time remember the power of a unit we taught years ago. We know which lessons tend to help students understand a difficult concept. But just because a cycle of lessons worked in the past with another group of students does not mean it will work well in the present with this group of children.

We also may inherit lessons from others. We take over the classroom of a teacher who has left a full file cabinet for us. We become part of a school community in which certain units of study have become traditions. There are many reasons why we may go back to lesson cycles that have worked in the past.

Revisiting past teaching as part of planning is important. Predicting how students may respond based on past experiences with other students is critical. However, that should be only one aspect of planning. We need to take into account our current students, new resources, and new understandings about student learning.

Not only that, but every lesson builds on the skills, strategies, and behaviors students already have in place. No unit stands alone. Even in a nonfiction lesson cycle, students bring their fiction-reading lives to the table.

When we think about the idea that no cycle stands alone, we can't merely think about the year that we work with students. Growing our readers across grade levels is just as important as growing them across a single year.

Rethinking the Study of Nonfiction

I was reminded of this when I planned a nonfiction Web reading cycle for my fourth-grade students. My original concern was that my students were merely skimming and scanning nonfiction. They were unable to build meaning, and often merely looked for games and videos online. They became easily frustrated with the layout of a website when trying to understand how it worked.

When I think back to my past teaching connected to nonfiction reading, I often (no matter the grade) did a unit on nonfiction text features. We worked for a few weeks identifying and exploring the features in nonfiction text such as labels, diagrams, and glossaries. I thought I could tweak this lesson series a bit to make it work for Web reading. I figured we could look at the text features that make Web reading unique and go from there.

Observations and Informal Assessments

I started to observe the students in their nonfiction reading—both on and off the Web. Students were *very* interested in nonfiction topics.

They are naturally curious, and want to access interesting information. I noticed that kids would choose nonfiction books, but when they sat down with them during independent reading time, many would merely browse the pictures and not read the text.

Students were doing very little cover-to-cover nonfiction reading. Instead, they browsed nonfiction for hours on end, never really digging into texts.

I soon realized that many students had experience with lessons on nonfiction text features—they could name and identify them—but their understanding often stopped there. I listened in as students made sense of nonfiction texts. They were consistently making incorrect inferences when they were confused. Instead of using multiple reading strategies to find answers or clear up confusion, they often made things up. There was little connection to them between the text and visuals. They were not skilled at putting information from text and images together to make sense of what they were reading.

I also realized that many kids did not have the same stamina for reading nonfiction that they did for reading fiction.

When reading websites, they were experts at finding games, videos, and unrelated advertisements. Many students immediately browsed for an activity when visiting a new site, rather than making sense of the information presented.

Students were honest about their frustrations with nonfiction when I talked with them. Several told me that they were good at watching videos and exploring websites for entertainment, but that it was hard to read online. I saw the same patterns whether students were reading a book, reading a website, or watching an informational video.

I started from scratch and abandoned the idea of tweaking lessons I had always used. I started by asking myself these questions to determine how best to meet student needs as nonfiction readers:

How does Web reading fit into the bigger picture of living life as a reader?
What does each group/child already have in place? What can I build on?
How do my students currently approach Web reading?
How do they currently approach other nonfiction reading?
Which needed skills cross over to other areas of reading?

Does it make sense to teach Web reading as a single unit of
  study? Does Web reading stand alone?
What is it that these kids need right now to become better
  readers of nonfiction text?
Can I do a cycle of lessons that will help students approach not
  only website reading differently, but all forms of nonfiction
  in a different way?

After reflecting on all I had learned from observing my students, I
determined that this was ultimately a stamina issue. Students did not
have the skills, strategies, or behaviors to stick with nonfiction long
enough to understand it. They became easily frustrated, skimming and
scanning. They created their own information or gave up quickly.
Without the stamina for reading and making sense of nonfiction text,
no other teaching would matter.

Nonfiction Teaching Now

There is no question that we need to rethink the work we have tradi-
tionally done with nonfiction texts. The days are over when we could
do a single nonfiction unit of study, or when we could embed all of our
nonfiction reading work into the content areas.

Years ago in a workshop, Regie Routman asked us to jot down
everything we'd read in a twenty-four hour period. The list helped me
see that even though I thought I was primarily a fiction reader, nonfiction was really what I spent the bulk of my time reading. Much of our
days are filled with nonfiction text. When I think back to the workshop
with Regie, I realize how long ago it was. The Internet was not part of
our daily lives. I can only imagine how much of our students' reading
lives focus on nonfiction texts now.

Much of what I read now is on the web with links, multimedia, and
social components that weren't available even a few years ago. The
whole idea of nonfiction text is expanding, and there are many ways
kids can access information. With the Common Core, the role of nonfiction text for students at all ages expands.

Technology is also expanding our students' lives as readers. Much
of their nonfiction reading is Web based, and we can only imagine the
new types of reading they may need to do in the future.

When I reflect on what I want for my students as nonfiction readers, I have to take into account all of the ways literacy has been expanded, and all of the new ways our kids have to experience nonfiction. It isn't enough to read nonfiction books. I want them to be able to pull information from a variety of sources, read with depth, synthesize the information they find, and be critical readers of information.

Nonfiction is difficult for many students. When I observed my students, I realize that I often did my lessons on nonfiction text features and then jumped right ahead and taught them how to judge the source or take notes. I never focused on building stamina to dig into nonfiction, to read beneath the surface, or to put the pieces together to be critical readers.

Another important thing I realized as I was planning this lesson cycle is that the Internet is merely a medium for nonfiction. As a Web reader, you need to do what you do with most nonfiction: make sense of the organization and features, and understand how they work together. There are so many different types of nonfiction (biography, documentary, news articles, how-to articles) that making sense of the organization and the way the text features work together is crucial. Later I will move on to judging the source and more sophisticated analysis, but first I want my students to read nonfiction for understanding.

Some experts seem to blame the Internet's wealth of information for the fact that many of us no longer read deeply. But instead of using that as an excuse, we must work to teach children how to read deeply. I agree completely with Nicholas Carr, author of *The Shallows: What the Internet Is Doing to Our Brains*, when he wrote, "As important as it is to be able to find lots of information quickly, what's even more important is to be able to think deeply about the information once we've found it. We need to slow down" (2010, 8). If we truly believe this, we need to take time to help children learn the skills and strategies necessary to do it.

More Than Just Features

Rethinking my nonfiction lessons forced me to look at many things. I realized that I could "teach" the lesson cycle I had planned, one that I thought had worked so well in the past, or I could create a new one that better met the needs of these readers. Rethinking lessons we've always done takes a great deal of time, but for me, the process is well worth it.

I came away with a new plan for a two-week cycle on building stamina for nonfiction. I realized that with these eight lessons, I could help students see the value in digging deeper into nonfiction. Recognizing that one lesson cycle in nonfiction reading is no longer enough, I know that this one will be the beginning of a yearlong study of reading nonfiction text. This cycle is designed to build stamina and give kids strategies for reading beyond the surface level. I also know that this cycle will allow me to see where to go next with these nonfiction readers. Much is built into the lessons that allows me to observe their skills and strategies.

Figure 3 Rethinking a Lesson Cycle You've Always Done

What is a lesson cycle you've done for many years or one that's been done in your school for many years?

Why do you think this is a set of lessons that needs rethinking? What isn't working?

Why do you teach it? What are your big goals? How does it fit into the big picture of reading skills for your students?

How do you assess the goals? Does your assessment match your goals?

What scaffolding may your students need to be successful with this?

How could you break this down for students?

What types of resources would help your students?

LESSON **Capturing New Thinking When Reading Nonfiction**

Nonfiction reading is a big part of our reading lives. Much of it is about adding new information and understanding to your knowledge base. Readers in grades 3–6 are interested in new information, but they are also interested in making correct predictions. This lesson places value on finding new information, and begins to build the idea that readers change thinking based on new information. It is important for students to attend to their own thinking while reading nonfiction, so a lesson like this one meets both goals.

Possible Anchor Text

I want several things in a text for this lesson. The text needs to be short enough for students to read in one sitting, but long enough to include lots of information to ponder. A book with stand-alone two-page spreads works well for a lesson like this where I model first, using one of the two-page spreads. A book I like for this lesson is *The Life and Times of the Ant* by Charles Micucci. This is one of a great series of nonfiction picture books that is packed with information. The author makes the topic interesting, there are several nonfiction features on one spread, and the topic is one that students are familiar with but probably don't know too much about. This leaves room for lots of strategic reading. One of my favorite pages to use is the one titled "Inside an Ant Hill."

How I Teach It

Although I have a teaching point in mind for this lesson, I also use it as an assessment. This lesson often guides me, letting me know where to go next. I want to see the kinds of thinking this particular group of students is comfortable with, and the skills and strategies they already have in place when dealing with nonfiction text.

I make sure that each child has a copy of the pages we are discussing, or I enlarge the text on a document camera so that each child can read it independently. I create a very traditional chart that is similar to a K-W-L chart with a few revisions. The first column asks kids to look at the heading of the page and to jot down what they already know. I give kids time to fill this out and then move on to the second column. (There is no sharing of this information, because it will affect the next task.) Before moving on, I let kids know that after we read, the second column will ask them to document new learning. As they read, they should mark the text to remember the new things they learn—whether they are brand new or changes in what they thought to be true. Although I don't want them to fill in the chart as they read, I want them to read with this purpose in mind. After the reading and time to fill out the chart, I ask kids to talk about new things they wonder, now that they know a bit more about ants and anthills.

During the lesson, I am listening to see how comfortable students are with monitoring their thinking, learning new information, and admitting when they learn something that challenges prior assumptions. My main message is that we think during nonfiction in the same ways we think while reading fiction. I also want to begin a conversation about valuing the learning of new information while reading.

Questions I Might Ask to Start the Conversation

What do you already know or think you know about this topic?

What are some new things you learned while reading?

Did anyone learn something that made you rethink what you thought you knew?

Is this a topic you are more or less interested in after reading about it?

What new questions do you have?

Follow-Up

The follow-up to this lesson would be based on inconsistencies I see in students' willingness to record thinking, document new learning, or change their thinking. Depending on what I noticed, I may need to back up and focus on just one area at a time. To do this, I could use other pages of *The Life and Times of the Ant* or another book from the series.

LESSON **Identifying Unknown Vocabulary**

No matter what nonfiction text we read, it is almost certain that we will come across new vocabulary. Being able to identify this unknown vocabulary as well as being able to use strategies to figure out the meaning of words is important to any type of reading, but especially nonfiction.

My main goal in this lesson is for students to begin to pay attention to and identify unknown words. I also want them to become aware that many words can be figured out with context clues, but some cannot. I may decide to create an entire cycle of lessons around nonfiction vocabulary based on student needs.

This skill of identifying unknown words is not specific to nonfiction reading. However, content-specific vocabulary is key to understanding a great deal of nonfiction text. I don't want students to skim and scan over unknown words. Instead, I want them to know that understanding vocabulary in the context of nonfiction reading is critical. I also want them to know when it is appropriate to skip an unknown word, and when readers need to dig a little deeper for meaning.

Possible Anchor Text

For this lesson, I want to find nonfiction text that has unfamiliar words that are easily defined by the context. I also want there to be some words that require other strategies.

A good book for this lesson is *Over and Under the Snow* by Kate Messner. This is a picture book that explores concepts of underground life. The book is told in narrative form. The author's note is critical for learning more about the subnivean zone, and the note includes a great deal of additional information as well as more new vocabulary.

The narrative portion of this text has some content-specific vocabulary, but it also has words within the narrative (such as *glide*) that students may not understand completely. The combination of words that may be familiar with those that may be completely new will spark a good conversation.

How I Teach It

I read aloud the book *Over and Under the Snow* by Kate Messner to the class. As I read, I have students use a sticky note to jot down words they aren't sure of. I pause at the end of each page so students would have time to jot down words.

After the reading, I ask students to revisit their lists, putting stars next to words that they "kind of know" and circling words that are totally new to them. As a class, we would chart the two types of words on the easel. Discussing similarities and differences is important, because I want students to understand that individual readers will have individual needs. We won't all have the same lists, and we all come to a piece with different backgrounds. Then we discuss the chart.

We revisit the pages where a few of the unknown words appear, and determine strategies for making sense of them. We often then sort the words into three categories (word meanings that can be determined by illustration, word meanings that can be determined by context, and word meanings that require outside sources for definition).

Questions I Might Ask to Start the Conversation

Which words are on your list that you've never heard?

Which words are words you've heard before but whose meaning you aren't sure of?

Which words are most interesting to you?

Which words are keeping you from understanding the text?

Which word meanings can you infer from the illustrations?

Which word meanings can you infer from the words and sentences on the page?

Which word meanings are impossible to determine without going to another source?

Follow-Up

I would follow up this lesson with posts from the website Wonderopolis. Wonderopolis posts a new inquiry each day. The variety of topics is one of many things I love about the site. By discussing an online piece, students can see that strategies for identifying unknown words are similar, but that the Web requires some Web-specific skills (such as clicking on links for unknown vocabulary).

I would also follow up this lesson by revisiting the charts we created throughout the study. Inviting students to use sticky notes to add their own words to the lists as they come upon them in independent reading will help them transfer the learning to their own personal reading. Sharing their findings with classmates will help them practice being aware of new words in their reading.

LESSON **Building Stamina—Continuing When a Text Gets Boring**

There will always be things we read that are not about topics we enjoy or that get boring for a few pages before capturing our interest again. Building stamina to "get through the boring parts" is critical for readers of nonfiction. I want my students to monitor their own level of engagement, and to know what to do if they notice their minds wandering. I also want them to realize that being aware of their engagement level might actually help them stay more engaged in their reading.

Understanding nonfiction—especially topics that are brand new to the reader—requires a high level of engagement. Readers also come to any topic with various levels of interest. I want my students to know that they have the skills and strategies to understand text about any topic—even if they aren't interested in it. But sometimes if you aren't interested in the topic, you need to work a little harder to keep reading.

Possible Anchor Text

I like to introduce this concept using a video. This meets my goal of expanding the types of information that are valued in the classroom. It also allows students to see that they can use the same strategies regardless of the format. Because videos take away the need for finding a reading level that works for everyone, they level the field a bit so that all students can participate.

One of my favorite sites for a lesson like this is Meet Me at the Corner (www.meetmeatthecorner.org), a website packed with short videos about places and people around the world. I like this site for lessons like this because the videos are short (typically four or five minutes) and interesting. Many of the videos would work for this lesson. The only thing that matters to me is that all students watch the same video so that we can discuss it more efficiently.

How I Teach It

I choose a video for students to watch and have them watch it on individual devices or as a group on the board. (Ideally, I like them to watch it individually so that they can pause the video as they jot notes, but either way works.) As they watch, I ask them to pay attention to times when they notice themselves getting bored and wanting to "change the channel" or stop viewing. At these points, I ask them to pay attention to their thinking, and to consider what made the video become boring all of a sudden. After the video, we gather to discuss what we've discovered. I know that many students will not participate fully in this discussion because they are not yet aware of their thinking patterns. But this conversation will launch the discussion, and we will still learn from each other.

Questions I Might Ask to Start the Conversation

At which point did you notice yourself losing interest?

Did you ever become interested again? Why or why not?

What did you notice yourself doing when you became disinterested? (Looking around the room, looking at other things on the website, daydreaming?)

How hard was it to refocus on the video? What did you do to help yourself?

Can you think of other times where you found yourself becoming engaged and then bored with a text, speaker, movie, or game?

Follow-Up

I want my students to see that engagement and sticking with something is a process they experience throughout their day, not only in reading. One thing I would do as a follow-up is ask them to record for homework times in their day when they notice themselves becoming bored. Coming back and talking about strategies they use for reengaging will be helpful when discussing nonfiction reading.

I might also do follow-up activities where I share a stack of books and ask students to determine which are topics that would be immediately engaging and which would take more work to become interested in. Holding up a book and asking this question will reinforce the idea that interest and determining what is "boring" is very personal, and will be different for all of us. The key is in knowing what is personally not interesting for you so you can develop new strategies for working with that type of information. Another related lesson idea is to share a table of contents with students, asking them to mark the sections that look most and least interesting to them.

LESSON **Text and Visuals Working Together**

It used to be that visuals were only a supplement to text in nonfiction pieces. As online information becomes more and more accessible, visual elements are becoming even more important. Instead of visuals being used merely to enhance information in the text, there is often a great deal of new information in visuals.

Often students can look at visuals and gather information, and read text for information. But combining visual information with text is sometimes a struggle for them. Over the years, I have noticed many elementary readers making incorrect inferences because they did not read the text that goes along with an image, or they did not look at a related image when reading text. Looking at all pieces of information before making an inference is critical to understanding many nonfiction texts.

Possible Anchor Text

I like to use sets of directions to introduce this idea. Often our students are familiar with this type of text because they use directions when building toys and games. This is also a genre where readers often go back and forth between text and visuals to make meaning.

For this lesson I look for sets of directions that have specific features. I want to talk to students about the idea that sometimes information is in the text only, sometimes it is shared in visuals only, and sometimes it is conveyed via both visuals and text. If I can find three sets of directions (cookbooks and cooking blogs are good sources) that show these three different things, that works well to introduce the lesson.

There are also books such as *See How It's Made* by Penny Smith in which text and photos work well together to share information.

How I Teach It

I begin this lesson by sharing (quickly) the three types of directions I've gathered. I show the students that sometimes information is told completely with visuals, sometimes it is shared with text only, and sometimes the two work together. Then I use a set of directions (enlarged so everyone can see) and do a think-aloud of my reading. A simple set of directions that uses text and visuals (preferably something with Legos or some other building toy that I can demonstrate as I read) is ideal.

I then think aloud as I read the directions to accomplish the task, making sure to show how I go back and forth from text to visual. I share when I am confused, and look at images for clarification. My goal is to make the point that the two types of information work together.

After the think-aloud, I ask students to discuss what they noticed me doing throughout the reading, and we create a chart with their comments.

Questions I Might Ask to Start the Conversation

What did you notice that I did to make sense of the directions? Are these things that you do?

What did I do in my reading that you might try in yours?

Can you think of things you read/see in which texts and images work together?

Do you tend to rely most on images or text?

How do you know when to go back and forth as I did?

Follow-Up

As a follow-up to this lesson, sending students on a search for nonfiction in which the visuals and text work together is a good way to help them internalize this idea. I want them to see that in some pieces, the visual is an added bonus, and in others, the visuals are critical and hold much of the meaning. By searching through nonfiction books and pieces, students can begin to determine when the visual elements and the text are meant to work together. This gives them practice so that they can use the same strategy in their own reading. If needed, I could create a chart highlighting the things students discover in their search.

LESSON Revisiting Text Features: Why Did the Author Do That?

Using text features well requires that our students understand the purpose behind an author's choices. This lesson is designed to help them see that the author intends for each and every text feature to help the reader make sense of the information.

As text becomes more sophisticated, the need to use a variety of text features in nonfiction reading grows. We are no longer able to assume that nonfiction text includes certain features. Instead, a reader must interact with the text to understand why the author used specific features to present information. I want my students to realize that these features are part of the craft of nonfiction writing. I want them to understand that these features are not "extras" but instead are crucial components.

Possible Anchor Text

I like to use books with stand-alone pages and lots of different text features for this lesson. I especially like two books by Michael J. Rosen, *Balls!* And *Balls! Round 2*. Both of these books focus on sports and the balls that players use. Each is packed with interesting information, and the features on each page are engaging. Diagrams, graphs, photos, and more are used to help the reader make sense of the information.

How I Teach It

This lesson has been most successful in a shared-reading setting where students can see a copy of the text, either on a board or with each student having a copy of his or her own. I identify a few pages that have different features (a diagram of the inside of a ball, a graph that is represented within an illustration, a caption of a photo) and take time to share each one.

I read the piece aloud, and we look at the feature together. I ask, "Why would the author include this? How does this specific feature help readers understand the information more clearly?"

Questions I Might Ask to Start the Conversation

When might an author decide to use a diagram?

When would a graph help the reader?

Why might an author use or not use a table of contents or an index?

What type of book/article/website might include a map? Why?

How much attention do you pay to the nonfiction features when reading?

Which features do you study, and which do you skim over?

Follow-Up

To transfer this idea to more complex texts, I might read aloud (over several days) one of the amazing texts in the Scientist in the Field series. Each book tells the story of one type of scientist and the problem they are solving. The books are designed to be read cover to cover, and there are many text features embedded throughout. This would be a great text for extending class conversations, because each day's read-aloud would most likely introduce a new feature in the book.

LESSON Layout and Navigation: Nonfiction Books

When beginning a new piece of nonfiction, it is important for readers to determine the organization of the piece and how best to navigate it. I want students to know that each piece of nonfiction is unique, and that authors use different features to help the reader better understand information.

Nonfiction text features have always been part of our study of nonfiction. However, often students could identify the features but couldn't use them to gain understanding. This lesson assumes that students know a bit about text features and have been in classrooms where these features have been introduced. For students to be able to read and understand nonfiction text, they need to be able to use the features offered in a text and understand the role of each one. By taking time to make sense of a text's organization and features, a reader goes into the text better prepared to understand.

Possible Anchor Text

This lesson requires a very large stack of nonfiction books (thirty to fifty). I want to choose a variety of books that show many ways that nonfiction can be organized, including narrative nonfiction that you would read cover to cover, encyclopedia-type books organized alphabetically, and books that have various features (table of contents, index, maps, photos, illustrations, graphs, and tables). There is nothing in particular I am looking for, except that I want the stack to have a huge amount of variety in terms of organization.

How I Teach It

This lesson is a collaborative activity for students. I put students at tables with a stack of books at each table. Then I ask them to pair up and look at one of the books on their table to determine how a book is organized, which text features that author has decided to use, and how a reader might go about reading it. I have sticky notes on each table so students can jot their thinking about the organization on the cover of each book before passing it along to the next pair of students. Each pair can add thinking to previous sticky notes.

Students then come together as a class to share the things they noticed. The teaching in this part of the lesson is key to understanding, and the questions below lead the conversation.

Questions I Might Ask to Start the Conversation

Was there a book on your stack that surprised you because of the way it was organized? Explain.

Were there any books that were meant to be read cover to cover? What do these types of books have in common?

How did you determine which books were meant to be read cover to cover and which were meant to be read in a different way?

Did anyone find a unique feature in a book—a feature we haven't discussed?

Was there a feature that was present in every single book you looked at?

Which type of nonfiction books appeal most to you? Do you tend to read nonfiction that is written to be read cover to cover, or do you like nonfiction that gives you more flexibility as a reader?

Follow-Up

For a follow-up to this lesson, I'd invite students to choose two nonfiction books and compare the ways in which the author used text features in each one. By actually reading the books and moving beyond the preview, readers can better understand the author's use of text features.

If necessary, I would do a few think-alouds with some unique nonfiction texts as I prepare to read them. I'd share my thinking with students as I made sense of the organization of a few books.

LESSON **Layout and Navigation: Websites**

Much of what our students read and will read in the future will be online. Making sense of the way that a website is organized is an important skill for students to have so they can access information online. This lesson is a natural follow-up to the previous lesson on navigating nonfiction texts.

If we want our students to be proficient readers of nonfiction, we cannot ignore online sources. Navigating nonfiction information online requires unique skills, and the ways in which readers can gain information changes daily. Making sense of online information is important, and the skills will transfer to any type of text.

Possible Anchor Text

I like to use a website such as DOGONews (www.dogonews.com) for this lesson. DOGONews is a site created especially for children, and it is packed with a variety of nonfiction information. It is easy to get lost in this website, so understanding the way it is organized is crucial when looking for specific information. The site uses tabs to organize big categories, topic tags to organize by topic, visuals, and connected links, and includes extra "fun" features such as quizzes. The site is challenging but accessible for upper elementary readers.

How I Teach It

I do this lesson as a think-aloud and project the website onto a screen so that all students can see it. I've spent time paying attention to the ways I navigate new websites so that I can share that process with students. I usually begin by taking a look at the homepage of the site and think aloud that I notice the tabs on top. I click on each of those, and think aloud about what I notice about each section. Then I go back to the homepage and note the topics on the side, clicking on a few of those to notice what each one takes me to. Then I go back to the homepage and scroll down the list of featured articles, thinking aloud as I go.

Finally, I scan down the right side of the page, looking at comments and other extra features that don't really get at the main information. I share/think aloud that I'd ignore that part of the site for now. I write on a chart the things I learned about the way this particular site is organized.

Questions I Might Ask to Start the Conversation

What do you notice about the way I tried to make sense of this site?
What did I do that you might try next time you access a new site?

What is challenging for you as a reader when you visit a new site?
How did I determine what was important and what I could ignore at the site?
Did you notice how I kept going back and forth from the homepage? Why do you think I did that?
Did you notice anything about the site that I didn't notice?
Is this a site you'd revisit in your free reading time? Why or why not?

Follow-Up

As a follow-up I would ask students to go to another site such as National Geographic for Kids (http://kids.nationalgeographic.com/kids/) and do the same type of exploration with a partner, summarizing their findings. We'd collect that information on a chart as a class and discuss it.

LESSON When to Skim or Scan and When to Read Deeply

Throughout this unit, the focus is on close reading, but there are times when skimming and scanning nonfiction is a smarter move. Our students may know how to scan for a fact, but knowing when it is appropriate to scan longer texts and when it is important to read closely is an important strategy they need to practice.

Sometimes deep understanding is not the goal of nonfiction reading. Readers may just need a quick bit of information that can be gained by skimming and scanning. For true understanding, I want my students to know the difference between skimming and close reading. I need to acknowledge the value in skimming and scanning to help them become authentic readers of nonfiction.

Possible Anchor Text

For this lesson, I would look for a short nonfiction book with a table of contents and/or an index. I like Nic Bishop's books because they are crafted well and are engaging to students. These books are packed with information and intended to be read cover to cover, but they each have an index, which makes them perfect for this lesson. One of my favorite Nic Bishop books is *Lizards*, which I would use for this lesson.

How I Teach It

Before the lesson begins, I prepare a list of questions on a chart to share with the students, including the following:

> How many types of lizards are there?
> Where do lizards live?
> What do lizards eat?
> Are lizards cold-blooded or warm-blooded?
> How are lizard babies born?
> What does a lizard need to survive?
> How do lizards protect themselves?
> Do lizards have claws?

We look at the chart together and think about how best to find the answers to these questions. The starred questions are those that can be answered by using the index and scanning the page referenced. The others need closer reading. Eventually, I want students to see that *how* and *why* questions often require close reading, and questions that need a one-word answer or number response are often best found when skimming and scanning.

We then go through each question and brainstorm the list of words we might use when searching the index. Using the index, we'd find the page and scan quickly for the answer. (This lesson could later be used to build Internet search/keyword skills.)

Questions I Might Ask to Start the Conversation

> What do you notice about the questions that require close reading?
> How do you decide when to skim and scan, and when to read closely?
> How do you know what types of words to look for in the index when searching?
> How do you go about skimming once you get to a page? Do you go from top to bottom? Look for bold words?

Follow-Up

A good follow-up to this lesson is to help students practice asking and answering different types of questions. By brainstorming questions that require close reading, as well as questions that can best be answered by skimming and scanning, students begin to see the purpose of skimming and scanning, and when close reading is a better choice. For follow-up lessons, students can work to brainstorm questions that might be answered in a book or article, categorizing them as appropriate for close reading or skimming and scanning.

CHAPTER 5

Reclaiming
the Joy *in* Planning

I believe that this corporate machinery of scripted programs, comprehen-
sion worksheets (reproducibles, handouts, printables, whatever you want
to call them), computer-based incentive packages, and test practice cur-
riculum facilitates a solid bottom-line for the companies that sell them,
and give schools proof they can point to that they are using every avail-
able resource to teach reading, but these efforts are doomed to fail a
large number of students because they leave out the most important
factor. When you take a forklift and shovel off the programs, under-
neath it all is a child reading a book.

—Donalyn Miller

Regardless of the messages we are getting from the media and politi-
cians, there is no one easy way to plan high-quality instruction for students. There is no one program, kit, or plan that will meet the needs of
every student in every school in the United States. Data should inform
our planning, not dictate our practice.

Teachers have always understood this. We know that planning needs to be thoughtful and purposeful, and that we must tailor instruction to meet the needs of our current students.

I may be overly optimistic, but I believe it is possible to teach thoughtfully and joyfully in this time of standards, mandates, and testing. We need to regain confidence in our ability to plan. I do this by knowing the standards and mandates, knowing what resources are available, and most important, knowing my students well. These three things will always be essential for thoughtful planning.

Planning for me used to involve sitting down and filling a plan book, creating bulletin boards, and making charts. Now my planning process includes lots of time reading new books so that I know children's literature well. My planning time is spent looking over assessment data and reflecting on classroom conversations. I also spend time going back into standards documents, so that I can understand deeply what it is my students should know. I spread out materials at the table or on the floor and spend hours looking over all that I have available to me. Planning takes time, but it is time that I love. Planning is at the heart of all that I do as a teacher.

Up to this point in the book, you have seen only the finished products of my planning along with a summary of my thinking, semi-neatly packaged. But planning is a messy process. I don't answer my own questions in the same sequence each time. I don't start with the children and move to curriculum each time. I'm not always sure of where to go in my thinking. My planning process varies depending on my comfort level with the topic or my knowledge of resources. But what remains true are my beliefs about minilessons, the questions I ask myself while planning, and the ways in which I go from big-picture to individual lesson planning.

I love this part of the planning process—the beginning. I love sitting down and thinking about all the possibilities and then narrowing things to best meet the needs of students. But it is never neat and tidy.

I am thinking about these upcoming lesson cycles. Here are my starting points for different lessons, to give you a time sense of the messiness of the process.

Figurative Language

This is a lesson cycle I enjoy. I have thought a lot about how to transfer understanding of words to reading comprehension. Over the years, I have collected books and resources that focus on words and word learning, so I know that I will begin with the resources. I'll look through the books I've collected as I sit with the standards to see which best match the things I need to teach.

My challenge in this cycle is that the students are coming to it with little or no vocabulary for conversations. This cycle is more of a test-prep study than anything else. These are skills that will be tested on our state test this spring, and I want my students to be prepared. However, I want more than that for our students. I want them to put these skills to use in the context of real reading and writing. This is the challenge with the planning in this study—how to make it authentic and embedded in real reading and writing.

Setting

I am a character reader. A lesson cycle on characters was easy for me, but I am not as comfortable exploring settings. I don't always see the point, and I need to be honest with myself about it. I am tempted to teach setting too quickly, just letting kids know that setting is about time and place. But I know there is more to it than that. So, I'll start this planning by revisiting books that might help me understand the role of setting a bit more deeply. I'll revisit Carol Jago's chapter on setting in her book *Classics in the Classroom*, and I'll revisit Kelly Gallagher's book *Deeper Reading*. These two experts will help me make better sense of the topic of this study. Some books are already coming to my mind that might fit well into this cycle. I am starting a stack that could change once I learn more. But right now, I have pulled *The Other Side* by Jacqueline Woodson, *Blackout* by John Rocco, *All the Places to Love* by Patricia MacLachlan, *Flora's Very Windy Day* by Jeanne Birdsall, and *Stellaluna* by Janell Cannon.

Annotating Text Online

A third cycle I am planning is one on annotating text online. Web reading is something that is becoming more and more important, but I have very little experience with teaching these skills, and there are few resources out there to help me. I won't be able to rely on picture books for this study. Instead, I'll need to find online resources that are accessible to elementary students. I am relying a great deal on my own learning and literacies while planning. I am paying close attention to the ways I annotate. I know my students will bring a great deal to this study. They know how to annotate text and to mark their thinking while they read. Much of this study will be about transferring these skills to online resources and learning strategies specific to Web-based reading.

Questions While Planning

For each of these lesson cycles, I have to not only identify the big goals I have for the study, but also revisit my beliefs throughout the process. I continuously ask myself the following questions during the planning process:

Do I have an end vision in mind? What are my big goals in this lesson cycle? Does each lesson build toward that vision?

Do I know the standards I am working toward? Do I know what strategies students have already that I am building upon? Do I have a wide range of resources to choose from as we move forward?

Have I scaffolded the lessons to build on past learning and on each other?

Are these lessons deep enough to continue to build on throughout the year?

Who is doing most of the working/talking/thinking when I look across the cycle—the teacher or the students?

What do I know about my current students that will affect the planning of this cycle?

Am I rushing things in this cycle to "get things covered," or am I stretching the lessons out even though students have an understanding of the content?

Do my lessons match the requirements for my district and state?

Are my lessons focused on the strategy, and not on any particular text? Am I assessing in a way that checks for bigger understanding of the concept rather than a "correct" answer?

Am I excited to learn how students will approach these lessons?

How willing am I to revise this plan as students respond differently from ways I've predicted they will?

In looking at my lesson cycles, I realize that there is no "right" style. Literacy is complex, and our lesson cycles will also be complex. It is impossible to talk about theme without also talking about inferring. It is impossible to talk about figurative language without talking about comprehension. When we get rid of the checklists that keep us moving in a quick and shallow way, we can plan thoughtfully.

I am hopeful that this book will not become another set of lessons for teachers to follow. By making my process visible, other teachers will be able to reflect on the planning processes that work for them. To find joy in our planning, we have to plan in a way that allows us to bring ourselves to the process—one that aligns with our beliefs.

It is easy to get caught up in the day-to-day work of teaching, and then be left with no energy for planning. But planning makes the teaching joyful and learning purposeful for our students.

The fun of planning is ultimately in the teaching. With the wedding planning that I wrote about at the beginning of the book, I was excited because I was planning a wedding. The big day was what mattered. The big day for us is every day that we have in the classroom with kids: we get to hear the thinking of our children and the learning as it happens.

BIBLIOGRAPHY

Alley, Z. 2008. *There's a Wolf at the Door.* New York: Roaring Brook Press.

Allington, R. 2011. *What Really Matters for Struggling Readers: Designing Research-Based Programs.* Boston: Allyn and Bacon.

Baker, J. 2002. *Window.* New York: Walker Children's Books.

Blume, J. 2002. *The Pain and the Great One.* New York: Atheneum/Richard Jackson Books.

Bennett, S. 2007. *That Workshop Book: New Systems and Structures for Classrooms That Read, Write, and Think.* Portsmouth: Heinemann.

Birdsall, J. 2010. *Flora's Very Windy Day.* New York: Clarion Books.

Bishop, N. 2010. *Lizards.* New York: Scholastic Nonfiction.

Brand, M. 2004. *Word Savvy.* Portland, ME: Stenhouse.

Brennan-Nelson, D. and Rosemarie Brennan. 2011. *Willow.* Ann Arbor, MI: Sleeping Bear Press

Brett, J. 1999. *The Gingerbread Baby.* New York: Penguin.

———. 1989. *The Mitten.* New York: Penguin.

———. 1987. *Goldilocks and the Three Bears.* New York: Putnam & Grosset.

Brisson, P. 2000. *Wanda's Roses.* Honesdale, PA: Boyds Mills Press.

———. 1999. *The Summer My Father Was Ten.* Honesdale, PA: Boyds Mills Press.

Brown, M. 1954. *Cinderella.* New York: Simon and Schuster.

Brown, P. 2006. *Chowder.* New York: Little, Brown Young Readers.

Browne, A. 2001. *Voices in the Park.* London: DK Children.

Bruel, N. 2008. *Who Is Melvin Bubble?* New York: Roaring Brook Press.

Buckner, A. "Teaching Themes Through Keywords." *Choice Literacy.* Choice Literacy, n.d. Web. 8 May 2012. <http://www.choiceliteracy.com/articles-detail-view.php?id=378 >.

Calkins, L. 1994. *The Art of Teaching Writing*. Portsmouth, NH: Heinemann.

Cannon, J. 1993. *Stellaluna*. New York: Scholastic.

Carmi, G. 2006. *A Circle of Friends*. Long Island City, NY: Star Bright Books.

Carr, N. 2011. *The Shallows: What the Internet Is Doing to Our Brains*. New York: W. W. Norton and Company.

———. "Is the Internet Making Us Quick but Shallow?" cnn.com. CNN, Web. 11 May 2011.

Chen, CZ. 2008. *Artie and Julie*. Alhambra, CA: Heryin Books.

Clark, R. 2004. *The Essential 55: An Award-Winning Educator's Rules for Discovering the Successful Student in Every Child*. New York: Hyperion.

Conroy, F. 1998. *Body and Soul*. New York: Random House.

Cooper, H. 1999. *Pumpkin Soup*. New York: Farrar, Straus and Giroux.

Creech, S. 2000. *The Wanderer*. New York: HarperCollins.

Dotlich, R. K. 2009. *Bella & Bean*. New York: Atheneum.

Fletcher, R. 2006. *Moving Day*. Honesdale: Wordsong Poetry.

Fox, M. 2009. *The Goblin and the Empty Chair*. New York: Beach Lane Books.

———. 2006. *Whoever You Are*. New York: Houghton Mifflin Harcourt.

———. 1989. *Wilfrid Gordon McDonald Partridge*. San Diego: Kane/Miller.

Fox, M. J. 2010. *A Funny Thing Happened on the Way to the Future*. New York: Hyperion.

Frazee, M. 2006. *Walk On!* New York: Houghton Mifflin Harcourt.

Fullan, M. 2009. *Motion Leadership: The Skinny on Becoming Change Savvy*. Thousand Oaks, CA: Corwin.

Gallagher, K. 2009. *Readicide*. Portland, ME: Stenhouse.

———. 2004. *Deeper Reading*. Portland, ME: Stenhouse.

Heide, F. P. 2009. *The One and Only Marigold*. New York: Schwartz and Wade.

Henkes, K. 1996. *Lilly's Purple Plastic Purse*. New York: Scholastic.

Hornsey, C. 2007. *Why Do I Have to Eat Off the Floor?* New York: Walker Books for Young Readers.

Jago, C. 2004. *Classics in the Classroom: Designing Accessible Literature Lessons*. Portsmouth, NH: Heinemann.

Keller, L. 2003. *Arnie, the Doughnut*. New York: Henry Holt.

LaMarche, J. 2009. *Lost and Found: Three Dog Stories*. San Francisco: Chronicle.

Litwin, E. 2010. *Pete the Cat: I Love My White Shoes*. New York: HarperCollins.

Lovell, P. 2001. *Stand Tall, Molly Lou Melon*. New York: Putnam.

MacLachlan, P. 1994. *All the Places to Love*. New York: HarperCollins.

McDonnell, P. 2008. *South*. New York: Hachette.

Marshall, J. 1989. *The Three Little Pigs*. New York: Penguin.

Messner, K. 2011. *Over and Under the Snow*. San Francisco: Chronicle.

Micucci, C. 2006. *The Life and Times of the Ant*. London: Sandpiper.

Miller, D. 2008. *Teaching with Intention*. Portland, ME: Stenhouse.

O'Connor, J. 2009. *Fancy Nancy: Splendiferous Christmas*. New York: HarperCollins.

Park, F., and G. Park. 2000. *The Royal Bee*. Honesdale, PA: Boyds Mills.

Park, L. S. 2011. *A Long Walk to Water.* New York: Houghton Mifflin Harcourt.

Parkhurst, C. 2004. *The Dogs of Babel: A Novel.* New York: Bay Back Books.

Pattou, E. 2001. *Mrs. Spitzer's Garden.* New York: Harcourt.

Piper, W., and L. Long. 2005. *The Little Engine That Could.* New York: Philomel.

Ray, Katie. "What Are You Thinking?" *Educational Leadership* 64.2 (2006): 58–62.

Rocco, J. 2011. *Blackout.* New York: Hyperion.

Rosen, M. J. 2008. *Balls! Round 2.* Minneapolis: Darby Creek.

———. 2006. *Balls!* Minneapolis: Darby Creek.

Rosenthal, A. K. 2011. *Plant a Kiss.* New York: HarperCollins.

Rosoff, M. 2008. *Meet Wild Boars.* New York: Square Fish.

———. 2008. *Wild Boars Cook.* New York: Henry Holt.

Say, A. 2003. *Emma's Rug.* London: Sandpiper.

Scieszka, J. 2009. *Trucktown!* New York: Simon and Schuster.

———. 1996. *The True Story of the Three Little Pigs.* New York: Puffin.

Smith, P. 2007. *See How It's Made.* London: DK Children.

Spinelli, J. 2004. *Wringer.* New York: HarperTeen.

Stegner, W. 1987. *Crossing to Safety.* New York: Penguin.

Thompson, T. "Are You Scaffolding or Rescuing?" *Choice Literacy.* Choice Literacy, n.d. Web. 8 May 2012. <http://www.choiceliteracy.com/articles-detail-view.php?id=735>.

Tolstoy, A. 1993. *The Great Big Enormous Turnip.* London: Sandpiper.

Van Dusen, C. 2011. *King Hugo's Huge Ego.* Somerville, MA: Candlewick.

Watt, M. 2009. *Chester.* Toronto: Kids Can Press.

———. 2008. *Scaredy Squirrel.* Toronto: Kids Can Press.

Willems, M. 2010. *City Dog, Country Frog.* New York: Hyperion.

———. 2007. *Today I Will Fly!* New York: Hyperion.

Woodson, J. 2001. *The Other Side.* New York: Putnam Juvenile.

Yolen, J. 2001. *Dear Mother, Dear Daughter.* Honesdale, PA: Wordsong/Boyds Mills Press

Series

Keene, C. Nancy Drew. New York: Simon and Schuster.

Andrews, V. C. Flowers in the Attic. New York: Simon and Schuster.

Willems, M. Elephant and Piggie. New York: Hyperion.

Rylant, C. Henry and Mudge. New York: Simon Spotlight.

Child, L. Charlie and Lola. New York: Grosset and Dunlap.

Willems, M. Pigeon. New York: Hyperion.

Wells, R. Max and Ruby. New York: Grosset and Dunlap.

Brown, M. Arthur. New York: Little, Brown.

Dewdney, A. Llama, Llama. New York: Viking.

O'Connor, J. Fancy Nancy. New York: HarperCollins.

Magazines

National Geographic Kids. Washington, DC.
Sports Illustrated Kids. New York.

Websites

Wonderopolis. http://www.wonderopolis.org.
Meet Me at the Corner. http://meetmeatthecorner.org.
Dogo News. http://www.dogonews.com.
National Geographic Kids. http://www.kids.nationalgeographic.com.

17732677R00052

Made in the USA
Lexington, KY
24 September 2012